S0-CFI-128

# SHAKER
## STYLE

# SHAKER
## STYLE

### MICHAEL HORSHAM

A QUINTET BOOK

Published in the USA 1996 by JG Press.
Distributed by World Publications, Inc.

The JG Press imprint is a trademark of
JG Press, Inc.
455 Somerset Avenue
North Dighton, MA 02764

This edition produced for sale in the USA, its
territories and dependencies only.

Copyright © 1989 Quintet Publishing Limited.
All rights reserved. No part of this publication
may be reproduced, stored in a retrieval system
or transmitted in any form or by any means,
electronic, mechanical, photocopying, recording
or otherwise, without the permission of the
copyright holder.

ISBN 1-57215-177-3

This book was designed and produced by
Quintet Publishing Limited
6 Blundell Street
London N7 9BH

Creative Director: Peter Bridgewater
Designer: Sara Nunan
Project Editor: Henrietta Wilkinson
Artwork: Danny McBride
Picture Researcher: Liz Eddison

Typeset in Great Britain by
Central Southern Typesetters, Eastbourne
Manufactured in Hong Kong by
Regent Publishing Services Limited
Printed in Singapore by
Star Standard Industries (Pte) Ltd

# CONTENTS

# INTRODUCTION

**LEFT** *The Horse Barn,
Hancock, Massachusetts.
Shaker architecture can
often, as here, be seen to
be a hybrid of almost
classical proportions
with traditional,
vernacular building
techniques.*

The presence of the art of the Shakers in the lexicon of design is not undeserved, but it is nonetheless strange. Shaker design did not spring from an adherence to the dictates of fashion, or from the impetus to exploit a market, but from a religious philosophy that wholeheartedly rejected the values of the world at large. Shakerism was a divinely inspired experiment in communal living; almost by accident it generated a genre of designs which have since attained the status of 'art objects'. Ultimately, Shakerism as a faith was to decline. Although some Shaker brethren and sisters survive today, they number fewer than a dozen and no longer conduct themselves with the same exclusivity practised by their forebears. It is significant that the Shakers' principal legacy to the world today lies not in their unique system of worship, nor in their egalitarian approach to communal living, but in the objects that the Shaker craftsmen and women created. These artefacts have transcended time and tell their own stories. The Shaker makers believed that they were working within the sight of God and that God was all-seeing. Therefore the same care was taken with the inside of a drawer as with the outside. The backs of chairs had the same standard of finishing as the fronts. All work was performed to the glory of God, and, in the Shaker object, it shows.

Upon their arrival in the New World, the Shakers were faced with the task of building their own environment. The completeness that characterizes Shaker settlements, the unity of vision and execution in everything from the humblest oval box to the round barn at Hancock, Massachusetts, or the characteristic granite-built meeting houses in other settlements, is an expression of the way Shakerism grew up and realized itself and its philosophies. Shakers literally created their world around them, with the watchwords propriety, purity and utility as their guides. That today the Shaker object is considered to be beautiful and desirable and can fetch high prices at auction is a testament to the perspicacity of the Shaker designer-makers. In appropriating current vernacular styles for their early furniture and architecture while eschewing the use of unnecessary ornament, the Shakers unwittingly forged the basis of a new aesthetic. The character of chairs and other pieces of furniture made by the Shakers was augmented by the exclusion of the worldly conceits of fashion and vanity.

**RIGHT** *A Shaker interior. This room exhibits many typical Shaker features, among them the pegboard, used for storing almost anything on the wall.*

8

Some 120 years in advance of Mies van der Rohe, the idea that 'less is more' was encapsulated by the Shaker maxims 'beauty rests in utility' and 'every force evolves a form'. In spite of being taken up by a fashionable élite in mid-19th century New York, Shaker furniture survived its subsequent abandonment perhaps because it was never created to pander to vanity, fashion and the vagaries of the civilized world. Shaker design came from a world studiedly apart from that of the everyday American in the late 18th and 19th centuries.

Nevertheless, the Shaker communities, as they grew, were forced more and more into interaction with 'the world' in order to ensure some kind of survival. Trade in furniture, brooms, seeds, preserves and other sundries bloomed in the early part of the 19th century, only to be hit 50 years later by the American Civil War. By the mid-to late 19th century the Shaker sect was markedly in decline, with membership falling through a lack of recruits, and the rule of celibacy preventing the creation of a new Shaker

**BELOW** *A detail from the alphabet board of the schoolhouse, New Lebanon, New York.*

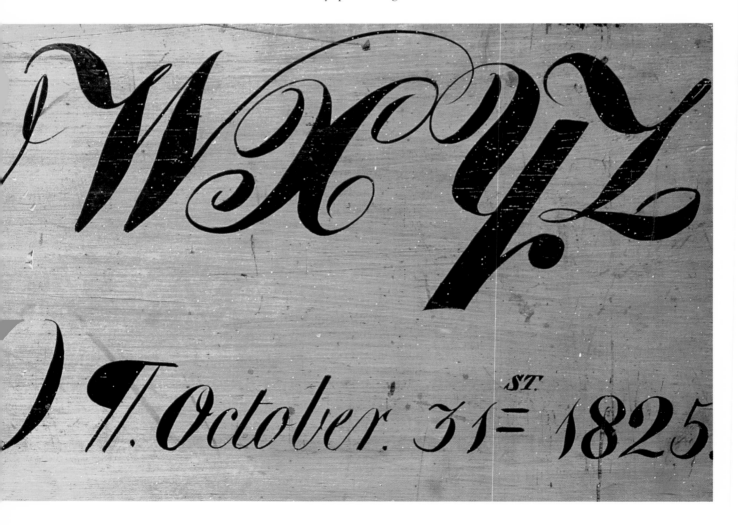

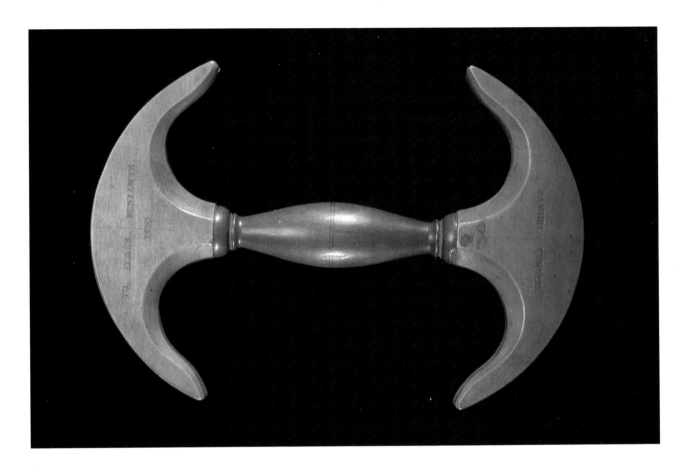

**ABOVE** *From New Lebanon, New York.*

generation from within. In retrospect, it can be seen that the Shakers were probably doomed from an early point in their history. Naïvety over money matters and several land transactions of a questionable nature cemented the physical demise of the sect as a practical example of communal egalitarianism. Yet, spiritually, Shakerism is still extant. It can be found in the early Shaker objects, the chairs, the buildings which bear testimony to work carried out in the spirit of the common good. These are things crafted by hands steadied with the Shakers' surety of faith in their destiny as the chosen people. 'Shaker' today exists as a name for a style. Enshrined within museums and auction houses and sold from shops with a designer bent, the vernacular tradition purified by the philosophies of Mother Ann Lee is proving to be increasingly popular once more.

The origins of the Shaker movement were nothing if not ignominious. The England deserted by Ann Lee was one of squalor and destitution for the majority of the population. Living and working conditions in cities such as Manchester, the birthplace of Mother Ann, were appalling. In spite of improvements to the city brought about by legislation such as the Cleaning and Lighting Act of

1765, disease still ran rife with waves of untreatable epidemics decimating the population. Housing in the rapidly growing conurbations of the north was inadequate for the influx of people who would work in the mills of the ever-growing cotton industry. The first canal of industrial significance linking Manchester with the coalfields had been opened in 1759, halving the cost of coal at a stroke and helping to pave the way for the industrial surge which was to follow. As the secular interests of industry grew, so the spiritual needs of the community at large were neglected. Manchester in 1750 had only one parish church serving a population of over 20,000.

However, by now the Anglican Church was not the primary institution for worship in north-west England. There was already a tradition of religious dissent and Nonconformity in this, and other parts of industrial England. So while Manchester was little more than a 'festering mill town,' there were fortuitous circumstances in the accident of birth that placed Mistress Lee in 'the little wen'. By the time she had reached maturity, dissent from the Anglican method of worship was the norm, characterized by the personality cults surrounding John Wesley and his Methodists and Robert Barclay, a prime mover in the spread of Quakerism. The campaigns of the Lancashire Dissenters for improvements in social conditions obviously made an impression on Ann Lee's young mind, as did the conditions within the mills, the streets and the town in general. Given the wretched conditions in the city and the hopelessness of her lot as a working-class girl, it is not too surprising that Ann Lee focused on the idea of a new existence away from the daily grind of life in a northern mill town. The circumstances which took her to America owe much to her faith, her campaigning, and the fact that, in mid-18th-century England, the Borough of Manchester was run on the lines of a baronial constituency by a handful of magistrates who ruled over their 'hundreds' with impunity and a predisposition for the harsh sentencing of those who would step out of line.

**LEFT** *Mother Ann's grave, near Albany, New York. The grave of the leading figure of the Shaker movement was a place of great significance for Shaker bretheren and sisters; in earlier times the headstone would form the centrepiece of ritualistic dances.*

13

# 1

## THE GIFT
## TO BE
## SIMPLE

The Origins of the
Shakers and their
Philosophy

**LEFT** *A knit carpet,
1890–95, attributed to
craftsmen at Hancock,
New Hampshire.*

In July 1772, Justice Peter Mainwaring, a physician by trade and a Justice of the Peace for the Borough of Manchester, tried a group of people at the Mole Inn, Toad Street, Manchester. The crime was 'Breach of the Sabbath'. On 20 July the same year the following appeared in the *Manchester Mercury:* 'Saturday last ended the Quarter Sessions, when John Townley, John Jackson, Betty Lees and Anne Lee (Shakers), for going into Christ Church in Manchester and there wilfully and contemptuously in the time of divine service, disturbing the congregation then assembled at morning prayers in the said church, were severally fined £20 each.' In the year of Our Lord 1772, £20 was a not inconsiderable sum of money, the equivalent of over £1,000 today. Obviously there was little hope that Ann Lee and the others could find such large amounts. Ann Lee was the illiterate daughter of a blacksmith, and a sometime millworker, hat cutter and washerwoman. The others in the group were either blacksmiths or of indeterminate trade. The only alternative to paying the fine was incarceration and Ann Lee, along with her confederates, duly found herself behind bars.

This was not the first time that Ann Lee's declared faith in Shakerism had led her into conflict with the law. The England of the mid-18th century allowed religious dissent and to a large extent tolerated worship outside the Anglican Church while still mistrusting the practices and trappings of Popery. The Quakers were one such dissenting sect. James and Jane Wardley (or Wardlaw) of Bolton-on-the-Moors seceded from the established methods

ABOVE *The towns of Manchester and Salford in the mid-18th century.*

of worship used by the Quakers and proclaimed themselves 'Shaking Quakers' in 1747. The name came from the paroxysms with which worshippers were seized when their religious fervour reached a critical level. The whirling, leaping and shaking which followed caused them to gain what was initially a derisive epithet. However, the name stuck and the 'Shakers' were born. Ann Lee did not join the sect until 1758 when she was 22 years of age. By this time James and Jane Wardley were well known in the locale as Shakers. They differed most strongly from the Quakers in that they followed the Adventist message of the French Camisards, prophets who had first opened their testimony in England as early as 1706 from having fled France and persecution in the years following the revocation of the Edict of Nantes in 1685. It was their unstinting belief in the second coming of Christ, together with the 'further degree of light and power' gleaned from Monsieur du Plán's Camisards, that set the Wardleys, and later Ann Lee, apart from the Society of Friends.

As well as being seen to be apart from the Quakers in particular,

**BELOW** *An early 19th-century Quaker meeting. Some of the Quaker traditions, such as gathering for prayer in a building specifically designed for that purpose, were continued by the breakaway Shaker group once they left mainstream Quaker practices.*

LEFT *A rare portrait of Ann Lee, 'the foundress of Shakerism'; it reveals little of her fabled charisma or alleged beauty.*

many of whom were respected businessmen and pillars of the community, the Shakers were at a remove from society in general, a characteristic that was to stay with them throughout their subsequent development. With their 'singing and dancing, shaking and shouting, speaking with new tongues and prophesying', the sect was mistrusted and even suspected of witchcraft and other dark practices. The arrival of Ann Lee in a town or village often provoked violence or a hue and cry, and several times 'Mother Ann' was attacked by those who considered the Shaker philosophy to be close to heresy. These early events formed the basis of, and became the breeding ground for, legends concerning the divinity of Mother Ann. Unfortunately for all its power, her supposed divinity offered her little protection against suspicion and hostility. Shielded by what she would claim was the Holy Spirit within her from the effects of violence, but not from the law of the land, Ann Lee often found herself in prison.

After her failure to pay the fine levied against her by Justice Mainwaring in the assizes at the Mole Inn in Manchester, Ann Lee was thus forced to spend what was to be her last term in an English gaol. It was there that she had a vision of a utopian society at peace in the New World. During this vision Ann Lee reached the conclusion that the root of all worldly evil lay in copulation. For her, the solution to the problem of sin lay in celibacy and in order. The vision of a community making its place in the new Israel of the American colonies beckoned to Ann Lee, and upon her release from prison she set about organizing a group of followers to accompany her to salvation in the New World.

Not a great deal is known of Ann Lee the person, save for her obvious charisma, which enabled her to lead eight people to America and keep them with her while they fought to set up the first Shaker settlement against what must have seemed insurmountable odds. Mother Ann was turned into a demi-deity by the subsequent Shaker communities, and legends about her abound. Just before she set sail for America with her small group of followers in 1774, Ann was hauled before a group of learned ministers in order to account for her allegedly heretical practices and beliefs. Shaker legend has it that she proceeded to confound the ministers of the Anglican Church by 'speaking in tongues'. Estimates of the number vary from 12 to 72, but it seems that the different languages were all delivered to such a degree of perfection that the ministers ended their examination of the witness by offering her a job as a teacher!

Setting sail for New York from Liverpool docks on 10 May 1774 aboard the ship *Mariah*, Ann Lee had with her eight followers;

among them were her younger brother William Lee; her husband
Abraham Stanley, a blacksmith; and James Whittaker, a distant
relation. Nearing the end of its three-and-a-half-month voyage
the little ship sprang a leak. All hands were called to the pumps;
a plank in the ship's side had lost its caulking and come adrift.
Water was flooding in, and the captain feared for the ship and the
lives of his crew and passengers. At this opportune moment, as
the story goes, Ann Lee had a vision of an angel, who assured her
that they would not perish, but would survive to reach their
'promised land'. Seconds later, a huge wave crashed into the side
of the stricken ship, forcing the plank back into place where it
could be made secure. The water was pumped out of the hold and
the ship sailed safely on. On Saturday 6 August the ship docked
in New York, delivering the Shakers to their new home. For non-
Believers, the provenance of the apocryphal legends surrounding
Ann Lee is dubious, but the credence attached to them by the
subsequently founded Shaker communities contributed to the idea
that her philosophies were divinely inspired and not merely the
heretical ramblings of a misguided if charismatic Englishwoman.
The *Summary View of the Millennial Church*, published in the early
19th century, has this to say about the beloved Mother Ann:

SHE WAS RATHER BELOW THE COMMON STATURE OF WOMAN, THICKSET BUT
STRAIGHT AND OTHERWISE WELL PROPORTIONED AND REGULAR IN FORM AND
FEATURE. HER COMPLEXION WAS LIGHT AND FAIR, HER EYES WERE BLUE BUT
KEEN AND PENETRATING; HER COUNTENANCE MILD AND EXPRESSIVE BUT
GRAVE AND SOLEMN. HER MANNERS WERE PLAIN SIMPLE AND EASY. BY MANY
OF THE WORLD WHO SAW HER WITHOUT PREJUDICE SHE WAS CALLED BEAUTI-
FUL, AND TO HER FAITHFUL CHILDREN SHE APPEARED TO POSSESS A DEGREE
OF DIGNIFIED BEAUTY AND HEAVENLY LOVE WHICH THEY HAD NEVER BEFORE
DISCOVERED AMONG MORTALS.

**BELOW** *The busy trading port of Liverpool, gateway to the New World, in the 18th century.*

LIVERPOOL IN 1728.

**ABOVE** *The Meeting House at Hancock, Massachusetts. Among the first of the meeting houses to be built, this design was taken from the original house erected at New Lebanon, later known as Mount Lebanon, in the early 1780s.*

What is clear is that she would have needed all of these qualities to maintain interest and morale among her followers in the early days of their life in Columbia County. Upon arrival, the group had to split up and find work in order to support themselves. Ann Lee returned to the life of a washerwoman and at times was so poor that she could not even buy her supper. Her husband, perhaps tiring of her commitment to a celibate life, left her, and the outlook for the Shakers must have seemed bleak indeed.

Throughout this time Ann Lee maintained both her faith and that of her small group of followers, until in 1776 they were able to buy a small tract of land at Niskeyuna, or Watervliet, near Albany, New York. This land was to form the basis for the first Shaker settlement, and in 1779 the first communal dwelling house was built. But injury was heaped upon disappointment when this house burned down shortly after completion. After five years in the New World the Shakers had not attracted any new converts, and with the departure of Mother Ann's husband the sect had actually declined in numbers. Furthermore, Mother Ann had attracted attention and was scrutinized as a possible English spy. America was at war with England over independence and the colonies were not always the best place to be, particularly for an English religious zealot. Nevertheless, Ann Lee continued to receive visions and visitations and assured her followers that one day people would 'flock like doves to the windows'.

In 1780, the turning point in the fortunes of the Shakers was reached with a religious revival that occurred along the north-eastern seaboard. Adventists in various parts of the north-eastern states were convinced that the second coming had taken place in the New World, and a fundament of Shakerism was the belief in the second coming of Christ. Mother Ann had convinced one Joseph Meacham, a Baptist minister, of the soundness of her own particular theology in a day-long meeting between his Baptist flock and the Shakers at Watervliet. Meacham in turn convinced many of his congregation that Mother Ann had the answers to the problems that had beset mankind since the Fall, and duly joined her, bringing many of his people with him. At last it seemed that Mother Ann's prophesying was to prove correct and that the Shakers were indeed destined to create a new order in a new land.

From 1781 to 1783 Mother Ann travelled through the northern states spreading the word of Shakerism. The doctrine of celibacy, separatism, confession and conversion must have been made to seem very appealing and its success can be seen as yet another testimony to the charisma of Ann Lee. This two-year journey resulted in the commitment to establish colonies of Believers at Harvard, Shirley and Hancock, Massachusetts, at Enfield, Connecticut, and at New Lebanon, New York. It also resulted in an attack upon Ann Lee, possibly because the native Americans suspected her of witchcraft or spying; both were equally heinous crimes in the eyes of the newly born American citizen.

Weakened by her travels and her travails, Mother Ann became ill upon her return to Watervliet and died there on 8 September 1784 at the age of 48. James Whittaker took over from her as the spiritual leader of the sect, and one of his first acts was to order the raising of the first meeting house at New Lebanon on 15 October 1785. By 1786 the building was complete and the first meeting in the church was at Christmas that year.

The next year James Whittaker himself died, leaving Joseph Meacham of the Enfield community to take over the running of the still-burgeoning sect. In September of that year he was joined in the leadership of the Shakers by Lucy Wright and the first gathering of the entire community took place as the United Society of Believers in the First and Second Appearance of Christ. The organization of the sect then proceeded apace with the verbal

# AN EARLY PLAN FOR THE SHAKER COMMUNITY AT CANTERBURY, NEW HAMPSHIRE

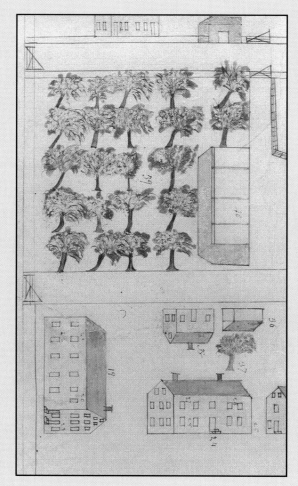

1

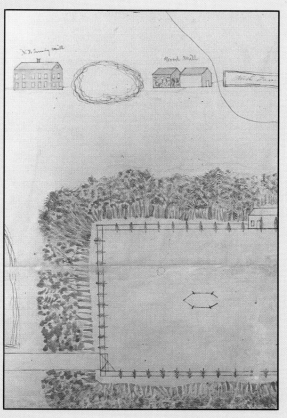

2

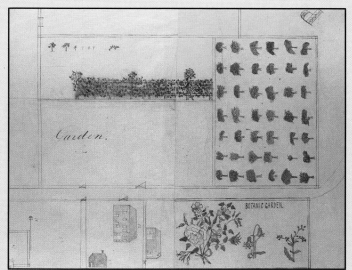

3

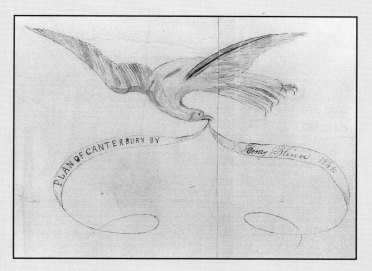

4

1 *The cover to a plan of the settlement at Canterbury. This drawing appears to have been inspired by the iconography of the* Holy Trinity, *which in fact played no part in Shaker theology.*

contracting of a covenant at New Lebanon in 1788. The following year the communities at Hancock, Massachusetts and Enfield, Connecticut were formally 'gathered to order', although the foundations for a meeting house at Hancock had actually been laid as early as August 1786. By 1791 the meeting house at Watervliet had been built, so cementing the organization started back in 1776. 1792 saw the community at New Lebanon 'called to Gospel Order with United interests', and it seemed as though Mother Ann's theology at last had a firm base from which to work. The Shaker Covenant was made in writing in 1795, and it is from this that much of the Shaker Order, or way of life, is derived.

The Shaker way of life depends on what is fundamentally a very simple philosophy; it revolves around equality, modesty, confession and faith. When, in 1808, Benjamin Youngs wrote *The Testimony of Christ's Second Appearing* commonly referred to

**BELOW** *Shaker chairs arranged for the union meeting. These meetings took place three times weekly and were the only times during which bretheren and sisters were allowed to talk without a definite purpose.*

as the Shaker Bible, much of Shaker order was contained therein. Then came the Millennial Laws in 1812. Such was the growth in the popularity of the Shaker way, with membership of the sect having risen from the original eight to 1,000 by the turn of the century, that laws became a necessity to ensure the harmony which was at the basis of their egalitarian approach to life. The Millennial Laws became the rule by which Shakers lived and covered every aspect of life in a Shaker community. They were laws that had been defined in the few short years that Shaker communities had been in existence and had been able to operate as self-sufficient enclaves within the broader independence of the Americas. As early as 1792 the community at New Lebanon boasted 214 inhabitants, 109 males and 105 females, with an average age of 24; clearly, rules had to be drawn up for the cohabitation of men and women in a celibate, communistic and egalitarian experimental community. The American constitution allowed for worship in whichever style the individual saw fit; the Shakers were then at liberty to crystalize their own peculiar brand of prayer and celebration.

The search for equality and unity eventually tempered the previously spectacular and individualistic displays of holy seizure. Early in Shaker history, the novice attending a Shaker meeting would often witness the sometimes disturbing sight of Shaker brethren and sisters 'coming under operations'. This might involve collapsing to the ground in a religious ecstacy 'turning', ie literally spinning on the spot, running around, convulsing, speaking or singing in tongues, and generally conveying union with the Holy Spirit by a display of the 'gifts of god', the Shaker term for divine inspirations. But this system of worship was not conducive to equality. The meeting would inevitably result in extravagant displays of divine intercession. How was the novitiate Shaker to feel but inhibited if surrounded by those well practised in the acceptance of the various 'gifts'?

The whirling gift, the gift of song, inspirational painting and the gift of verse represented only some of the facets of the Shaker religious experience. Coming under operations was seen to mark the first stage in the opening of the soul to the Lord, the first step on the road to full status as a Shaker brother or sister. With the habitual search for order and harmony enshrined as an essential part of everyday Shaker life, new forms of worship were devised in which a rigidly laid down pattern of dance steps was executed to the music provided by the principal singers of a Shaker 'family'. Dances such as the 'square order shuffle', the 'ring dance', and many other variations, were rehearsed during the week to be perfect for the Sunday worship. However, the steps were kept

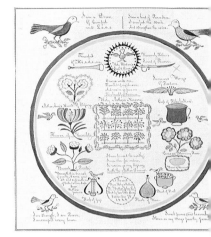

**ABOVE** *This spirit drawing, A Present from Holy Mother to Brother John C., September 7th, 1848, is attributed to Polly Ann 'Jane' Reed (1818–1881). She was a member of the Shaker family at New Lebanon, New York.*

simple so that everyone in the community could learn them. Practice was encouraged not for vanity's sake, but so that unity and commonality, symmetry, simplicity and perfection could be carried into every area of Shaker life, including the worship from which they had originally gained their name.

Away from the meeting house and apart from Sunday worship, the Shaker philosophy came to be characterized by calmness and order in everything with the routine of daily life devoted to the maintenance of the community and the living of the Shaker life to the full. At its zenith Shakerism captured the quintessence of a holistic and ordered approach to life. It is not surprising that it proved attractive to many people who, upon arriving in the New World, found themselves trying to make headway in what was, in parts, a barely civilized wilderness. The charisma of Mother Ann lived on. Although illiterate herself, she had coined some aphoristic maxims which would aid the Shaker brethren and sisters in defining their faith and living their lives. It seems that Mother Ann's followers had noted down her homespun philosophies and then included them in a 'Shaker constitution'. Her sayings placed the Shaker approach to life and work 'in a nutshell': 'If you can improve in one talent, God will give you more'; 'Put your hands to work and your hearts to God'; 'Do your work as though you had a thousand years to live and were to die tomorrow', and 'Trifles make perfection but perfection is no trifle'.

By the early years of the 19th century the Shaker sect was growing steadily and it seemed as though Ann Lee's prophesying was to come true. The Millennial Laws were there to maintain the precepts of Shakerism in the new communities that were springing from what had become the fountainhead of the faith, the Church Family at New Lebanon. Although Mother Ann's axiomatic approach to canonizing the Shaker philosophy was disseminated by the publication in 1816 of *The Testimonies of the Life, Character, Revelations and Doctrines of our ever Blessed Mother Ann Lee*, it was ultimately the Millennial Laws that fixed the stringent order by which the Shakers lived, updated every so often by the ministries and bishoprics which came to govern the running of the order.

Every aspect of daily life from rising to retiring was governed by these laws, and there was no leeway given for things which might lead to the love and re-adoption of 'worldly' practices. The laws stated that: 'No male and female shall support or have private union or correspondence together, neither shall they touch each other unnecessarily.' Further, the laws stated that it was 'contrary to orders' to 'kneel with the left knee first; to put the left boot or shoe on first; to kneel with handkerchief in hand; to put the left

**ABOVE** *Shaker bretheren and sisters photographed outside the Dwelling House at South Union, Kentucky, c1885. Although markedly in decline as a sect by this time, the Shakers continued to maintain rigid standards in dress and deportment.*

foot on the stairs when first ascending'. These brief extracts, although they come from a book purporting to be sensational, called *Shakerism Unmasked*, characterize the attention to detail which was to contribute to the search for perfection in the Shaker way of life. Attention to the small things was designed to affect the construction of the whole. All was directed towards plainness, which would extend to the adoption of plain speech, as in the Quaker sect, with 'yay' and 'nay' (but not 'thee' and 'thou') the order of the day. The idea of living a life without blemish, 'sound, pure, wholesome and free from error', was central to the essentially Christian philosophy followed by the Shakers. The achievement of purity through the establishment of a common bond was pursued in worship, in dress, in the buildings in which the Shakers lived, in the chairs upon which they sat and the desks at which they wrote. Underpinning this commonality was the vow to celibacy, the renouncement of personal ownership of goods and the shunning of the ways of the outside world. To be a Shaker was to redefine both the self as an individual and the place that the individual had in the world.

To be a Believer, as the Shakers came to refer to themselves, was to subjugate the self for the good of the whole, therefore any of the devices which the outside world would employ in order to proclaim status through goods or 'vain show' was discouraged and eventually forbidden by the Millennial Laws. Under the section 'Superfluities not Owned' it was declared that:

**ABOVE** *The Ministry Shop and Meeting House, Sabbathday Lake, Maine. This meeting house was built to the same specifications as the New Lebanon original.*

FANCY ARTICLES OF ANY KIND OR ARTICLES WHICH ARE SUPERFLUOUSLY FINISHED, TRIMMED OR ORNAMENTED, ARE NOT SUITABLE FOR BELIEVERS AND MAY NOT BE USED OR PURCHASED; AMONG WHICH ARE THE FOLLOWING; VIZ.

SILVER PENCILS; SILVER TOOTH PICKS; GOLD PENCILS, OR PENS; SILVER SPOONS, SILVER THIMBLES (BUT THIMBLES MAY BE LINED WITH SILVER); GOLD OR SILVER WATCHES; BRASS KNOBS, OR HANDLES OF ANY SIZE OR KIND; THREE BLADED KNIVES; KNIFE HANDLES WITH WRITING OR PICTURING UPON THEM; BONE OR HORN HANDLED KNIVES EXCEPT FOR POCKET KNIVES; BONE OR HORN SPOOLS; SUPERFLUOUS WHIPS, MARBLED TIN WARE, SUPERFLUOUS PAPER BOXES OF ANY KIND, GAY SILK HANDKERCHIEFS; GREEN VEILS; BOUGHT DARK COLOURED COTTON HANDKERCHIEFS, FOR SISTERS USE; CHECKED HANDKERCHIEFS MADE BY THE WORLD, MAY NOT BE BOUGHT FOR SISTERS USE EXCEPT HEAD HANDKERCHIEFS; LACE FOR CAP BORDERS, SUPERFLUOUS SUSPENDERS OF ANY KIND; WRITING DESKS MAY NOT BE USED BY THE COMMON MEMBERS; ONLY BY PERMISSION OF THE ELDERS. THE FOLLOWING ARTICLES ARE ALSO DEEMED IMPROPER, VIZ. SUPERFLUOUSLY FINISHED, OR FLOWERY PAINTED CLOCKS, BUREAUX OR LOOKING GLASSES; ALSO SUPERFLUOUSLY PAINTED OR FANCY SHAPED CARRIAGES, OR SLEIGHS, SUPERFLUOUSLY TRIMMED HARNESS AND MANY OTHER ARTICLES TOO NUMEROUS TO MENTION. THE FOREMENTIONED THINGS ARE AT PRESENT UTTERLY FORBIDDEN, BUT IF THE MINISTRY SEE FIT TO BRING IN ANY AMONG THE AFOREMENTIONED ARTI-CLES WHICH ARE NOT SUPERFLUOUSLY WROUGHT, THE ORDER PROHIBITING THE USE OF SUCH ARTICLE OR ARTICLES IS THEREBY REPEALED.

BELIEVERS MAY NOT IN ANY CASE MANUFACTURE FOR SALE, ANY ARTICLE OR ARTICLES WHICH ARE SUPERFLUOUSLY WROUGHT AND WHICH WOULD HAVE A TENDENCY TO FEED THE PRIDE AND VANITY OF MAN, OR SUCH AS WOULD NOT BE ADMISSABLE TO USE AMONG THEMSELVES, ON ACCOUNT OF THEIR SUPERFLUITY.

Despite the attempt at the eradication of staus-bearing commod-ities through the implementation of these laws, an organization as big as the Shakers needed some kind of hierarchy to facilitate the smooth-running of each community. It is estimated that by 1850 there were upwards of 6,000 members spread through some 18 communities. Nearby communities were governed by bishoprics formed from the ministries, which were in turn made up of elders and eldresses of certain 'families'. The ministry was a self-perpetuating governing body which had the power to elect the new members who were in essence the lawmakers for the Shakers. Each community, depending on its size, was divided into Families. Each Family had at its head an elder and an eldress who were in charge of the running and spiritual well-being of the dwelling in which they lived. Some of the older communities would have a further hierarchy built in, with the oldest Family referred to as the Church Family or Centre Family and the others defined by their geographic relation to the Church Family, ie East or West. As Shakerism continued and grew the complexity of its structure and its dealings with the outside world also increased until, in some ways, the Shaker experiment was at a far remove from its humble beginnings in the witnessing of simple acts of faith.

The early success of the Shakers led to an influx of potential new members, known as novitiates: soldiers from the Revolution army, workers from Scandinavia, Britain and other parts of Europe, together with some second-generation Americans. All were attracted by the relative security of the Shaker communities. The Shakers were willing to take any soul whose commitment could

**BELOW** *South Union, Kentucky, c1885. The Centre Family Dwelling (1824) and the Meeting House (1818) in the foreground. The Meeting House is brick built, as opposed to the more usual New Lebanon wooden prototype, reflecting the growing prosperity of the Shakers at the time of building.*

THE SHAKER.

be proven through their 'turning' to the Shaker faith. Thomas Brown, author of *The People Called Shakers* published in 1824, was one such novitiate. Lured by the simplicity of a life uncomplicated by marriage, sex, fashion and other worldly conceits, Thomas Brown attempted to join the Shakers but ultimately withdrew. His book recounts the process of Shaker meetings and the receipt of 'gifts' by the sisters and brethren and charts his own reaction to the process. During his narrative the author admits, 'At one time I had a gift to sing, but no one understood what I sung nor myself either.' Thomas Brown's main reasons for deciding not to join the sect came with the crisis of faith he felt when told by one elder that, in the past, some Shakers had received a gift to dance naked. Poor Thomas Brown could not reconcile the idea of a pure, celibate community with that of dancing naked in the meeting hall, and so withdrew from the sect in order to write his exposé of Shaker practices.

Thomas Brown's view of the Shakers as a sect indulging in practices contrary to the accepted Christian norm was not, however, shared by every commentator who came into contact with the Shaker way of life. Charles Nordhoff, in his book of 1859 *The Communistic Societies of the United States of America*, recounts his own experience of being received by the Shakers in one of their communal houses:

**ABOVE** *Shaker interior. Shaker rooms followed a similar pattern wherever they were built. The lack of excess in either the conception, execution or furnishing of the room creates an effect of unified restraint, warmth and utility.*

I FOUND MYSELF IN A COMFORTABLE, LOW CEILINGED ROOM WARMED BY AN AIRTIGHT STOVE, AND FURNISHED WITH A COT BED, HALF A DOZEN CHAIRS, A LARGE WOODEN SPITOON FILLED WITH SAWDUST, A LOOKING GLASS AND A TABLE. THE FLOOR WAS COVERED WITH STRIPS OF RAG CARPET, VERY NEAT AND OF A PRETTY QUIET COLOUR LOOSELY LAID DOWN. AGAINST THE WALL NEAR THE STOVE HUNG A DUSTPAN, SHOVEL, DUSTING BRUSH AND A SMALL BROOM. A DOOR OPENED INTO AN INNER ROOM WHICH CONTAINED ANOTHER BED AND CONVENIENCES FOR WASHING. A CLOSET IN THE WALL HELD MATCHES, SOAP AND OTHER ARTICLES. EVERYTHING WAS SCRUPULOUSLY NEAT AND CLEAN. ON THIS TABLE WERE LAID A NUMBER OF SHAKER BOOKS AND NEWSPAPERS. IN ONE CORNER OF THE ROOM WAS A BELL, USED AS I AFTERWARD DISCOVERED TO SUMMON THE VISITOR TO HIS MEALS. AS I LOOKED OUT OF THE WINDOW I PERCEIVED THE SASH WAS FITTED WITH SCREWS, BY MEANS OF WHICH THE WINDOWS COULD BE SECURED SO AS NOT TO RATTLE DURING STORMY WEATHER WHILE THE LOWER SASH OF ONE WINDOW WAS RAISED THREE OR FOUR INCHES AND A STRIP OF NEATLY FITTING PLANK WAS INSERTED IN THE OPENING – THIS ALLOWED VENTILATION BETWEEN THE UPPER AND LOWER SASHES THUS PREVENTING A DIRECT DRAUGHT WHILST SECURING FRESH AIR.

**BELOW** *The Schoolhouse at Canterbury, New Hampshire. Clapboard outer walls house the ubiquitous sash windows.*

The tone of Nordhoff's piece on the Shakers is laudatory. He is clearly impressed by the attention to detail in the fittings of the house in which he is staying and by the orderliness and cleanliness with which he is surrounded. This passage, and indeed the book in general, reveals a great deal about the Shaker way of life. The built-in cupboards; the Shaker books and newspapers; the cot beds, which were standard issue for all brethren and sisters; the fact that the rag carpets were loosely laid and never tacked down in order to facilitate the cleaning of the wooden floors; the general cleanliness: all these phenomena were endemic to the Shaker way, and symptomatic of their approach to life. Everything, to the Shaker communities, was a gift from God. One of the most famous proclamations of this idea is contained within the lyric of a song to which they used to perform their celebratory but worshipful dances:

> *'Tis the Gift to be simple*
> *'Tis the Gift to be free*
> *'Tis the Gift to come down where we are to be*
> *And when we find ourselves in the place just right*
> *'Twill be in the valley of love and delight.*
> *When true simplicity is gained*
> *To bow and to bend we shan't be ashamed*
> *To turn, turn will be our delight*
> *'Till by turning, turning we come round right.*

# 2

## THE
## SHAKER
## OBJECT

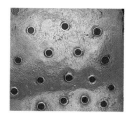

LEFT *Stacks of oval 'nice boxes'. A staple of the manufactures of many Shaker communities, the boxes' swallowtail construction can easily be seen.*

Shaker furniture, and Shaker objects in general, represent a meeting between the spiritual and the secular world. As a whole the manufacture of Shaker furniture was controlled by the adherence to Shaker philosophies governing work, superfluity and utility, but the appearance of the furniture was nonetheless conditioned by the craft traditions brought to the New World by the chair and cabinet makers who were the early recruits to the Shaker way. Many of the early converts to Shakerism, who were to define the style for future generations, were of Northern European extraction and were skilled in the vernacular techniques of their home countries. Even second-generation American Shakers would have learned their skills from a colonial settler. Therefore it is a relatively easy task to draw an evolutionary line to the basic furniture-making techniques employed by the early Shakers from those used in Europe prior to this time.

However, the furniture that might have been made by the honest 'bodger' in rural England, Sweden or the Americas differs in one crucial respect from the furniture that was made by the early Shakers, in that the impetus behind the making of the furniture had fundamentally changed by the time the ordinary carpenter had become Shaker carpenter. The Shaker carpenter was unequivocably working for the glory of his God. Yet, although Shaker carpenters were ostensibly distancing themselves from the art of surface decoration which could be found in the emergent American middle-class home, the conceits of craftsmanship remained in early Shaker work under the guise of Godly diligence. Shakers professed to have no need for grace and beauty in the furniture they made, preferring to allow the use to which it would be put to determine the form. 'Every force evolves a form', went the Shaker dictum. The fact that the Shakers believed in the penoptical abilities of their God meant that equal care was lavished on each part of the piece under construction. The absence of a sloppily turned finial or chair post is as characteristic of Shaker chairs as the care with which a bevel would be applied to a drawer front for a Shaker cabinet.

It was early Shaker furniture which most displayed these characteristics of hand-workmanship. Edward Deming Andrews, a leading authority on the Shakers, conveniently divided Shaker furniture production into three distinct phases: early, middle and late. The early period, from the inception of the first communities through to the first decade of the 19th century, produced furniture with the characteristics which have just been described. The reliance on hand-working skills was never more prominent than during this time. The middle period, from around 1810 to the American Civil War of 1861–65, saw the consolidation of the

**ABOVE** *A washstand. Simply and sturdily constructed, the washstand shows typical Shaker ingenuity with the positioning of the circular pail stand. This is hinged and can be swung out from under the basin to allow easier access to the pail containing the dirty water.*

Shaker idiom into a generic and easily recognized style while the beginnings of machine and rationalized batch production meant a reduction in the individual character of pieces which came out of the various communities. Although furniture emanating from New Lebanon or Watervliet would have details distinguishing it as the production of those workshops, the chairs, rockers and other pieces increasingly displayed fewer and fewer of the hallmarks of true craftsmanship. Turning marks from the lathes would be left on the chair posts while other tell-tale signs of machine production trumpeted the fact that although these were indeed Shaker pieces, they came from the surety of machine production and not the celebration of a single craftsman's belief in God. The late period, from the latter part of the 19th century onwards, is distinguished by a decline in Shaker furniture production as the communities wound down into decay and desertion. The average age of the inhabitants of the communes went up as new recruits to what was perceived as a dwindling order became harder and harder to find. The demand for new furniture in the existing settlements dropped and orders from the outside world became fewer, and the Shaker furniture industry all but died out.

Across the three periods in which the Shakers busied themselves with the production of goods for use and sale, several distinct types of furniture emerged as staples of an industry catering for local demands, while other types were reserved almost

**ABOVE** *Shaker shovel. This shovel was carved from a single piece of walnut, and while it follows American tradition, it is nevertheless a typically Shaker object in the standard of finish and the fineness of its proportion.*

**RIGHT** *A daybed in the Gathering Room at Hancock, Massachusetts. Note the broom and the writing tablet hanging upon the all-purpose pegboard.*

exclusively for the use of the Shaker brethren and sisters themselves. Perhaps the archetypal Shaker object is the side chair.
Simply constructed along the lines of all vernacular furniture, the
Shaker side chair formed the basic unit of production of the later
Shaker chair factories. When it was originally conceived, this
chair allowed for the expression of the Shaker faith in wood. In
effect, it became Shakerism extant. Slightly backward leaning,
for Shakers were not averse to a little comfort, and lightly but
sturdily constructed, the side chair was the epitome of Shaker
workmanship and utility. Materials used were culled from the
woodlands owned by the sect, and were selected for their strength
and lightness. Thus the chair posts would be made from seasoned
maple, a good hard wood with a generally straight grain, although
burr or birdseye variations of the same wood would also be used.
Other woods, such as cherry, birch and walnut (butternut), were
also used, but less often. All Shaker side chairs were made with
three slats at the back, the slats usually of maple because of its
resilience, and the rungs also of maple, or sometimes ash or
hickory. Splint of any pliant wood was used for the seating in
early chairs, but later leather, cane, tape and woven straw could
all be found as typical seating materials.

*ABOVE A Shaker side
chair. This example
exhibits all the common
traits of the Shaker side
chair – three slats in the
back, tilting feet on the
rear legs and rush
seating. The turned
finials at the top of the
rear posts are the
remaining traces of
traditional chairmaking
practice which Shaker
craftsmen brought with
them from the outside
world.*

The Shakers at New Lebanon saw chair-making for that area become almost the exclusive property of the Canaan and Second Families. James Farnum, Gilbert Avery and John Lockwood are known to have been instrumental in setting up the basis of what was to become, for a short time, a relatively prosperous industry. According to various commentators, the deterioration in traditional Shaker workmanship came with the American Civil War and the effect that the conflict had on the system of production used in many American manufacturing spheres. By 1863 a branch of the Second Family at New Lebanon had called itself into Gospel Order and had become an independent Family. The elders of this Family wasted no time in setting up a chair factory equipped with machinery such as wood and iron lathes, a boring machine, a planer and a dressing machine. The New Lebanon chair workshops moved further toward a factory system of production with the introduction of labour-saving machinery. The publication of a catalogue for the wholesale trade has been seen as a pandering to popular taste; at the very least it represented a dilution of the original Shaker ethos of exclusivity.

By 1868 the South House Family was selling in wholesale quantities to areas around Boston, Philadelphia and New York, with production running at about 600 chairs per year. In 1872

**RIGHT** *A chest of drawers. This chest has an unusual top with a folding leaf. Shakers were in favour of any device which could be stored away after use.*

another factory was erected to cope with demand and an investment was made to the order of $1,000 in an engine to drive the factory machinery. All this had been achieved under the leadership of elder Robert Wagan, who stood at the head of the South House Family at New Lebanon. In 1874 a further chair catalogue was issued by this Family. It was designed to capitalize on the advertising which these particular Shakers had been running in the newspapers of the eastern seaboard since 1865. Although it may seem that the maintenance of chair factories on this scale went against much of the Shaker doctrine, it should be remembered that the Civil War, as well as providing the technological means to scale up production, also disrupted what had until then been a very lucrative seed trade with the South. Clearly the Shakers had to find some way to fill the financial gap which had been left by the removal of half of their agricultural customers through the untimely intervention of war. Chairs proved to be the new staple for some Shaker communities, and the side chair was by no means the only variant.

One of the most simple yet effective Shaker inventions was the tilting foot. Attached to the back posts of the standard side chair by means of a ball and socket joint, the tilting foot allowed for the person seated to rock on to the back legs of the chair while keeping the back feet safely flat on the floor. The tilting foot saved many Shaker floors, which as well as being highly polished and therefore slippery were most often made of soft pine and were easily dented by a conventional chair being rocked in this fashion. So popular was the device that a patent was drawn up for a metal version in the 1850s by someone close to but outside the Shaker faith. Shakers did not go in for patenting their inventions, believing that patents led to monopolies, something of which they wanted no part. The chairs themselves, while popular with many Shakers, did cause questions to be asked within the Shaker movement about the propriety of rocking a chair in this way, and, worse, leaning against the walls in such a lazy fashion. Shakers may have been strict in many ways concerning the conduct of their daily lives but old habits were seen to die hard. The chairs continued to be made and the Shakers continued to rock on them. (In much the same way, the tobacco chewing habit was frowned upon by many Shakers, but although it was discouraged it was not forbidden. Oval spit boxes filled with sawdust and chippings were a common sight on the floors of retiring rooms.)

The side chair, with or without tilting feet, was most often used in the union meetings which occupied the Shaker brethren and sisters on the evening when there was no formalized 'dancing' worship. Equal numbers of brethren and sisters would meet in a

ABOVE *A swivel chair. Constructed entirely from hard woods, such as maple and hickory, these chairs drew on the construction techniques used in the traditional Windsor chair but represented an innovatory use of the wood turner's skill. They were used in the offices of various Shaker communities.*

OPPOSITE *A side chair and a child's chair. Fitness for purpose demanded that the adopted Shaker children could not be allowed to perch on the adult Shaker chair, so it was common for the youngsters to have chairs specially made for them. The sect's strict rules of celibacy meant that they had no children of their own.*

room with their side chairs ranged opposite each other a 'safe' distance away. The Believers of both sexes would then converse simply on matters concerning their faith and their work.

LEFT *A Shaker rocking chair. This is a typical example of a Shaker rocker. Four slats in the back and the neatly turned 'mushroom' posts on the arms are characteristic of many Shaker rocking chairs produced during the 19th century.*

The Shakers' penchant for rocking on their chairs was carried over into the development and manufacture of the rocking chair proper. Originally intended for use by elderly and infirm Believers, who would find the rocking motion soothing and beneficial, the rocking chair was soon to be found in every Shaker dwelling, usually in the retiring rooms of brethren and sisters alike. The most revered rocking chair in the whole of Shakerdom is to be found at Harvard, Massachusetts. There are few artefacts still existing whose provenance involves Mother Ann. Therefore Mother Ann's Chair is of special significance to the Shakers. The chair itself is unspectacular, yet unusual. It is not a true Shaker chair, in that it was not wholly constructed by the Shakers. It appears to be a standard New England Windsor chair converted into a rocking chair by the addition of sled rockers to the legs. The rockers are fashioned from a hardwood, probably maple, and then dowel-jointed on to the outside of the rather clumsily turned, splayed legs. The effect is unprepossessing, but, given that Mother Ann had a special relationship with the Harvard community and lived there for two years before her death, the chair takes on an aura of historical and religious importance for the Shakers.

ABOVE *Mother Ann's rocking chair, an item of particular significance for Shaker adherents.*

Other rocking chairs actually manufactured by the Shakers may not have had such an important past, but they are nonetheless important in the understanding of Shaker furniture as a whole. There are many variations. Some were manufactured with 'mushroom posts' at the ends of the gracefully curved arms, others sported scrolled or rolled arms, and later even cushioned arms. Materials used were the same as those used in the side chair, and the one trait which seems to link all Shaker rocking chairs is the use of four slats in the back.

It is generally accepted that the Shakers were the first producers in the New World of the rocking chair on a systematic scale. The lessons learnt from producing large numbers of chairs for new communities and 'the world' were applied to the production of the rocking chair as it became more and more popular among both Believers and people outside the sect. The success and the omnipresence of the rocking chair are further evidence of the Shakers' predisposition towards comfort. Their belief that it was a godly duty to avoid disease and maintain good health may well have had a lot to do with the use of rocking chairs for relaxation, and indeed for some types of work, for with typical pragmatism the Shakers developed the 'sewing rocker'. Specifically for use by sisters, the sewing rocker was shorter and manufactured without

ABOVE *A sewing desk,*
*originally built in*
*Alfred, Maine, and now*
*in a private collection.*

arms to allow easy access to the sewing basket which was kept by the side of the industrious user.

Chair production was not the only arm of Shaker furniture manufacture to flourish when the movement was at its peak. However, it was the only branch of the industry to be properly organized with a view to selling to the outside world and making a profit. The 'case furniture', or cabinets, trunks and chests of drawers, made by the Shaker brethren was largely designated for use by the Shakers themselves and did not find its way into the world in the same way as did the chairs. One class of case furniture built by Shaker craftsmen and never intended for use elsewhere was the built-in cabinets which still grace the rooms of Shaker dwellings. As much architectural details as pieces of furniture, these cupboards were used for storing anything from cutlery and crockery to candles and clothes. There exists a particularly fine example of built-in drawers in a workshop at the Hancock Community in Massachusetts. The cabinet features 48 separate drawers built into one wall. The drawers decrease in size toward the top of the cabinet, lending the whole in-built construction a sense of proportion which a simple exercise in symmetry would not have done. The graduation in drawer size also meant that heavy items would be placed nearer the bottom of the cabinet, a further example of Shaker practicality. Each drawer features a very simple ogee moulding and a central wooden knob. The end-grain of the knob has taken a darker lustre from the varnish than the drawer fronts proper and this serves to punctuate and emphasize the regimented and neatly realized design. The drawers were probably used to store herbs and medicinal plants in what was the pharmaceutical shop.

The Church Family Dwelling at Hancock also has fine examples of built-in furniture, with graduated drawer sizes and drawer fronts of walnut. The effect is one of harmony and utility. The chief architect of this building, William Deming, wrote: 'Scarcely a knot can be seen in all the work, except for the floors and they are yellow pine and are very good. There are a hundred large doors including outside and closet doors; 245 Cupboard doors – 369 drawers – these we placed in the corners of the rooms and by the sides of the chimneys . . . and I think that we may say that it is finished from the top to the bottom, handsomely stained inside with a bright orange color.' The system of building-in was by no means exclusive to the Shakers, but it suited the Shaker way because it eliminated the problem of dirt gathering around and on top of individual pieces of furniture. As Mother Ann had apparently often repeated, 'Clean your room well; for good spirits will not live where there is dirt. There is no dirt in heaven.'

The attic of the Church Famly Dwelling at Canterbury, New Hampshire was built in 1837. It features 6 closets, 14 cupboards and 101 drawers, all of which are numbered. It is entirely constructed from pine. Likewise the storage area in the Church Family Dwelling in Enfield, New Hampshire also contains an impressive number of built-in drawers, 860 in all. In 1875 in Sabbathday Lake in Main the Shaker community added a new roof to the ministry shop, which provided space for some more built-in storage space for the sisters. These sets of built-in drawers are unusual, being finished in a light grey paint with only the drawer pulls left in a natural wood finish.

Cabinet work carried out by Shaker carpenters was always characterized by a lightness and deftness of execution mingled with a fine attention to detail and propriety. Unlike the chair-manufacturing industry, the cabinet makers never had to scale up their production to cope with demand; there is therefore a consistency about their products, founded on the skilled hand-work that was carried out in the true spirit of the Shaker faith. Chests of drawers, blanket chests and storage chests all exemplify

ABOVE *A cupboard and case of drawers from New Lebanon, New York, c1825–50.*

the kind of cabinet work that was designed for domestic use and displayed Shaker traits. There are, however, some curious anomalies. A blanket chest made at Canaan, New York in 1837, for example, features bone escutcheons around the locks on each drawer. Locks were not a common feature on Shaker furniture, as the renouncement of personal ownership of goods obviated the need for security within the community. That this chest should feature locks, and decorated locks at that, is odd indeed.

Often the Shaker craftsmen would make specialized pieces for the sole use of certain members of the sect – small chests for tools, seeds or herbs. All such pieces were constructed with the same diligence, attention to detail and preoccupation with fitness for use.

Another specialized piece of case work was the woodbox, a workaday item designed to carry the wooden fuel for the Shakers' famous airtight stoves. They were lent a touch of ingenuity by the inclusion of a drawer at the bottom of each piece, designed to collect smaller pieces of wood and wood chips which could then be used as kindling. Each room containing a stove also had another wooden box, lidded this time, for storing tongs and shovels on hooks fixed to the sides. It was therefore a ubiquitous and utilitarian piece of furniture, but nonetheless it bore all the hallmarks of Shaker workmanship and inventiveness.

The stoves themselves deserve a mention, staples of Shaker manufacture as they were; although over 200 variations of airtight stoves have been recorded there are basically two types – the box stove and the panelled stove. They were manufactured in quantity and sold to the world from the settlements of Hancock and Mount Lebanon, but they were most often seen warming every room of the Shaker dwelling. Some versions included a pan on the top of the stove where water could be put to humidify the air. Other types included a second firebox or radiator above the primary firebox to generate more heat; these were known as double-deckers. The panelled stove was made from five plates bolted together to form the body, and differed from the box stove in that it sometimes featured cabriole legs and ball and claw feet. Panelled stoves were often made, in later years, outside the Shaker communities. In spite of their un-Shaker-like ornamented legs they were considered superior to the original and far simpler box stove.

The high cupboards and chests, which stood at 6 or 7ft (about 2m) and were most often found in the kitchens of dwelling houses, were accompanied by step stools of two, three and four steps depending on the size of the adjacent cupboard. Writing desks were to all intents and purposes almost badges of office, for it was not just any Shaker who had access to these pieces. The hierarch-

**ABOVE** *The Pharmacy at Hancock, Massachusetts. Built-in cupboards were often a feature in the Shaker shops or manufactures. The stencil on the window sill for the Shakers' patented hair restorer gives some indication of the diversity of their business interests – trade with 'the world' (Shaker terminology for all non-Shakers) was always acceptable.*

**RIGHT** *Shaker chest. Used for storage of blankets or rugs, the green stain was by no means unusual on Shaker furniture, as many different colours were used. Rather than being used simply for decoration, these colours were reflections of the way things were thought to be coloured in heaven.*

ical nature of Shaker society may seem at odds with their professed notions of equality and egality, but the fact that only certain elders and eldresses and members of the ministry could use writing desks meant that status, distance and, above all, authority was maintained. For a community to run successfully as a strictly controlled order in the way the Believers did for so many years, it was important that authority and the hierarchy within that order should be maintained.

The idea of manufacturing pieces of furniture for specific purposes was fundamental to the Shaker carpenters. Ironing tables, for instance, were sturdily constructed, for ironing was a demanding, hard task, carried out by the sisters and governed by its own set of laws. Every joint of the table was dowelled, and the table top was set upon two cruciform trestles, each of which was braced by stretchers tenoned into the legs. Cross braces ran underneath the top and were then morticed straight into the legs. Another guiding principle in Shaker cabinet-making was the desire for tidiness, and the habit of storing things away after use prompted the adoption and manufacture of the drop-leafed table as a Shaker

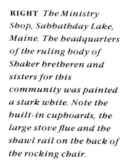

**LEFT** *A Shaker workstand. Optimum use of the work surface is ensured by the design of this piece which has drawers for small items bridging the worktop. This would also allow for lengths of material to be drawn through. The blue stain is common in Shaker furniture of all kinds.*

**RIGHT** *The Ministry Shop, Sabbathday Lake, Maine. The headquarters of the ruling body of Shaker bretheren and sisters for this community was painted a stark white. Note the built-in cupboards, the large stove flue and the shawl rail on the back of the rocking chair.*

staple. These tables appealed to the Shakers' sense of economy and neatness. Anything that could be folded away after use was seen to contribute to the Shaker ideal of a 'place for everything' and to general cleanliness. Ranging in size from 3–10ft (1–3m) long, these tables were used in every part of the dwelling. Retiring rooms, pantries, seed shops and infirmaries all benefited from what the Shakers saw as a space-saving addition to their furniture needs.

A table that was very much the product of the Shakers' characteristic inventiveness was the bread-cutting table. Strongly built from a hardwood, the bread-cutting table featured a knife cum guillotine designed to operate on a sliding pivot fixed to a rail on the back of the lipped top. The unleavened bread upon which the Shakers dined could thus be cut quickly, cleanly and efficiently. Speed was essential, with up to 200 diners at one sitting in some of the larger communities.

The brethren and sisters would dine in the same room but in monastic silence. They sat at dining tables constructed from long pine boards, closely jointed to allow for easy cleaning. No table linen was used, so the surface of the dining tables had to reflect the cleanliness that was such a part of the Shaker way of life. Dining tables were also designed to seat 'sets' of Shakers in groups of four. Thus a 12-foot (3.6m) dining table would seat 12 people in three groups. The division into these groups allowed food to be passed around without the need for speech: once more Shaker furniture can be seen to be an integral part of the smoothly running lifestyle of the Believers.

A smaller item of furniture produced by all Shaker cabinet makers was the stand, and various types were manufactured from the earliest days of the Believers' communities in the late 18th century. Designed to stand at the side of the rocking or side chair, these simple stands consisted of a round or square top and a drawer upon three splayed legs. Along with the side chair they are perhaps the oldest type of object made by the Shakers. With the chairs, tables and the chests they were regarded as part of the jointly owned flexible stock of furniture possessed by the Family, and would be put to a wide variety of uses.

**RIGHT** *The interior of the Ministry Shop, Canterbury, New Hampshire. Of particular interest in this otherwise typical Shaker room is the small work table on the left, with its lockable document chest and castored feet. Also note the bone handles on the cupboard doors.*

Materials, as we have seen, were generally drawn from the wooded lands owned by the Shakers; if there was a shortage of suitable wood it was bought in. All the woods used were hardwoods, fruitwoods or softwoods, with by far the most flexible and oft-used material being pine. However, lime, walnut, maple-rock, birds-eye and burr, cherry, birch, red beech, ash and hickory all make appearances in Shaker craftsmanship. Where the Shakers departed from what were seen as traditional treatments of wood was in the range of finishes they developed for application to completed pieces of furniture.

Colour played a large role in the definition of the Shaker aesthetic, and some colours, as in dress, had special meanings, such as white for purity and blue for virginity. Early furniture was often painted a deep red or ochre yellow. However, the finishes applied to the surfaces of pieces of furniture were as much a preservative measure as an aesthetic one. Indeed, the Millennial Laws of 1845 stated that only 'movable objects' were to be painted or varnished. But it is a mistake to assume that the Shakers were against ornament and that they championed dowdiness. The lightness of spirit and the joy that characterized their

**BELOW** *Shaker steps. Even the most simple objects, such as these steps, were products of care and skill in their design and manufacture; the steps were much needed to reach the top drawers of typical fitted cupboards.*

ABOVE *Shaker side table.
An early type of Shaker
table stained a light
yellow ochre.*

worship were carried over into the manufacture of their environment. Shaker furniture was, as it were, surrounded by the heavily
coloured and stylistically overblown furniture and décor of the
mid-to-late 19th century, and in that context the understatement
that is so characteristic of the Shaker idiom was at times inter-
preted as 'drabness'. Charles Dickens, for one, during his visit in
1842, had no time for what he perceived as the unimaginative
dryness of Shaker design.

The search for chemical certainty in the manufacture of dye-
stuffs for furniture was yet another facet of the preoccupation
with equality and harmony in all aspects of Shaker life. With
many Families drawing up guidelines for the decoration of their
dwellings, furniture and clothing, the Shakers moved ever closer
to the realization of Mother Ann's original scheme. Shaker furniture, both built-in and free-standing, was but a part of the struggle
to realize this vision. As the way of life lived by the Believers has
almost died out, the furniture is in some ways a window to the
time when the Shaker faith was in the ascendant. The hand-worked
artefact, the product of the Shaker 'shop' is a testament of faith
which in some cases is almost 200 years old. The 'hands to work
and hearts to God' approach of the Shaker craftsmen and women
is as evident in the form of these objects as is the meeting of the
vernacular traditions with what were new holistic philosophies
for the living of day-to-day life. As such, the importance of origi-

**RIGHT** *Detail of a skimmer, used during the cooking of large quantities of food for the bretheren and sisters. It would have been made entirely by hand, so reflecting, in its own way, the devotional aspects of all Shaker making.*

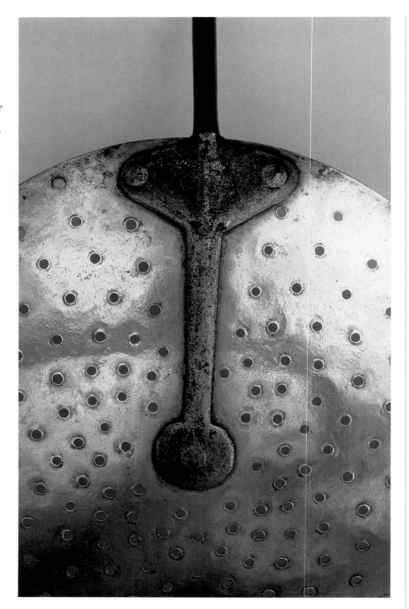

nal Shaker furniture as a historical phenomenon and a class of devotional object cannot be overestimated.

The devotional aspect of manufacture was not reserved for the furniture that emanated from the workshops of the Shaker communities across America. Other Shaker objects were often tinged with the same approach, whether they were made by the women in the sisters' shops for sale as fancy goods or by the men in the machine houses for wholesale to merchants in nearby towns. Systematic production of humble objects by the sisters in their manufactories or shops was often still by hand, therefore it is in these objects that the original Shaker idea of craftsmanship as a means of

**RIGHT** *Full view of the skimmer.*

**LEFT** *Two wooden pails. Pails like these would have been used all over the Shaker dwellings and farms, although the colouring of these particular objects suggests that they would have been used indoors rather than out. The close-fitting lids indicate that they might have been used for the storage of foodstuffs.*

worship survived longest. What are commonly called 'fancy goods' in contemporary sources and records – fans, baskets, shawls, bonnets, coloured woven tapes and a range of homely articles – were sold to what had become in many states a growing horde of tourists attracted to the spectacle of Shakerism. The advent of the railroad made Shaker communities more accessible to the world at large and vice versa: one community actually owned and leased a large brick-built hotel near the local railway station.

An archetypal Shaker object with a variety of uses was the oval box. Commonly called a 'nice box' when used for storage, this multi-purpose Shaker invention was also used for everything from herb store to spitoon. Used as the latter, larger versions of these receptacles would be filled with sawdust and placed in every

**BELOW** *Shaker mixing bowl. Turned from a single piece of wood, these bowls were common in the Shaker kitchens. However, earthenware bowls were relatively easy to come by in 'the world' and the Shakers often availed themselves of worldly goods such as crockery and cutlery.*

LEFT *Sawdust-filled spitoons standing on a woven rug in a typical Shaker room. The initials 'MR' on the left hand box probably stands for 'Meeting Room', while the number on the box on the right reflects the Shakers' passion for order. Note the towel rack, washstand and rocking chair in the background.*

corner of a room. Although the habit of chewing tobacco was discouraged by the elders, the spitoon came into its own when the meeting house doors were opened on Sundays to visitors wishing to observe the Shakers at worship. The boxes themselves are constructed from a hardwood case with a pine top and bottom. The wood would be bent around a form, and steamed or immersed in hot water; it would be kept on the form until dry. It was then tacked into place with pins. Iron or copper pins were used to fix the sides of the box, although copper proved more popular with the makers as it did not discolour the wood as it aged and oxidized. All boxes had swallowtails in one end of the single piece of maple or walnut that formed the sides. The swallowtail was cut from a template, and a knife was used rather than a jigsaw so that a bevel could be put on the edge of the swallowtail shape to increase

**ABOVE** *A covered wooden pail and 'nice box'. The staining of these objects in ochre and red reflects the passion the Shakers had for colour in their designs.*

its flexibility. The swallowtail was by no means a purely decorative device; it was intended to allow the box to move and 'breathe' under changes of humidity and temperature while retaining its shape. The boxes were usually made as ellipsoids, but circular boxes are not uncommon. Larger boxes could have handles fixed to them; they were then transformed into baskets for berries, herbs and roots. Another manifestation of the Shaker box was the dipper or dry measure used for the counting of grain, dried corn or fruit.

Many Shaker objects were made with the ubiquitous peg rail in mind. In all Shaker buildings, a peg rail was installed 6–7ft (1.8m–2.1m) from the floor as an integral part of the wall. At regular intervals of about 1ft (30cm) pegs were fixed to the rail so that anything that was not in use could be stored out of the way by

**RIGHT** *Interior, Canterbury, New Hampshire. The chair is hanging in its correct position, so that dust cannot gather on the seat and ruin clothes. The basket on the table is an every day example of one craft which was a staple of Shaker manufacture.*

RIGHT *A clock movement, probably by Benjamin or Isaac Youngs. Clockmaking within the Shaker communities represents yet another example of how skills learnt in 'the world' found their way into the Shaker movement.*

being hung up on the rail. Thus it was not uncommon to find chairs hanging up on a wall alongside a candle holder, clock or candle box. The candle holders themselves were typically utilitarian in design; often they were little more than a wooden tray which could take the candlestick with a stem rising from the back into which would be bored four or five holes which would allow the height of the candle to be changed. The candle could then be set lower if a Believer was sitting by a wall, reading by it and higher if it was to light a passageway or room.

Most of the clocks for the Shaker communities were made by either Benjamin Youngs or Isaac Youngs of Watervliet, or Calvin Wells the clockmaker at Canterbury who was himself once apprenticed to Benjamin Youngs. Benjamin Youngs, the author of *The Testimony of Christ's Second Appearing*, the so-called Shaker Bible, and one of the three men sent out to spread the Gospel around the time of the Kentucky revival in 1805, was also a renowned clockmaker, his favourite idiom being the long-case grandmother clock. These clocks would be made with a pine case and a hand-worked movement, both of which would display the characteristic Shaker traits of pride in workmanship coupled with propriety in execution. Unlike chair production, which was to succumb to the need for mass production, clockmaking was one area where factory production techniques seemed not to impinge on the way in which the Shakers worked. Although by the middle of the 19th century cheap clocks were easy to come by, the Shaker clockmakers continued the traditions learnt as apprentices well into the age of mass manufacture. Their adherence to the traditions of the 18th century meant that their religious faith could be expressed, as it had been at the beginning, in the perfection of timepieces that required consistently high standards of craftsmanship even to work, let alone to run for years.

Other clocks, those made principally by Isaac Youngs, were wall-hanging and used the peg rail. Consequently they could be moved from room to room, wherever they were needed. The clockmakers at Watervliet and Canterbury had eventually made an alarm clock for every Shaker community. The elders had realized

**RIGHT** *A long case clock. Made by Benjamin Youngs at Watervliet, the 'grandmother clock' proved to be the marriage of both clock- and cabinet-making skills.*

that the running of succesful communities required accurate time-keeping, but that watches, being expensive and a vanity, were contrary to order and should not be used. Communal movable clocks were the obvious answer and were readily adopted by all Shaker communities.

Such objects as the spinning wheel and the loom were not specific to the Shakers, but the Shaker versions of these objects were, like all their creations, influenced by their observance of the need for propriety and simplicity in all things. Therefore, while the ordinary spinning wheel might display the traits and conceits of worldly production techniques, with fancily turned spokes or perhaps some decorative carving, the Shaker spinning wheel was seen to be the model of stripped-down efficiency.

**BELOW** *A wall hanging clock. Designed to hang from the pegboard in any part of a dwelling or shop, this clock dated 1840, is proof that Shakers continued their handworked production techniques well into the age of mass-manufacture.*

**RIGHT** *Shaker spinning wheel. In an era where even the most mundane and utilitarian of objects were customarily decorated, the approach of the Shakers to the manufacture of their tools was consistent with their approach to furniture and architecture; beauty was seen to rest in utility.*

**BELOW** *Reels for holding the home-spun yarns which the early Shakers would use in their weave shops.*

Maple would be used for the wheel as it could be bent into the necessary circle. Spokes would be simply turned from maple and notably free of any decorative effect whatsoever. Furniture and tools such as these spinning wheels, yarn reels and table swifts (devices for winding wool from skeins into balls) were all treated as belonging to the same class of object by the Shakers who laboured in their construction. That is, everything produced by the Shakers was ostensibly functional. Whereas a more worldly person would expect finer workmanship on the objects which could be found, and admired, in a living space, the Shaker would work steadily and with the same degree of skill on whatever was put in front of him. This refusal to differentiate between the value of different objects by investing more labour in some than in others is what makes objects of true Shaker origin unique in conception and construction. In spite of their utilitarian appearance, they are quite literally 'not of this world'.

# 3

## SHAKER
## ARCHITECTURE

**LEFT** *Architecture at Canterbury, New Hampshire. The Dwelling House at Canterbury was erected around 1793 and exhibits detailing which is classical in inspiration. Note the carved urns at the ends of the balustrades in the foreground and the use of columns and triangular pediments.*

Shaker Architecture shares many of the features of Shaker furniture: it is the product of adaptation, vernacular skill and practical necessity.

The architecture of the New World in the late 18th century was a colonial version of contemporary European architecture. The Shakers eschewed ornament for ornament's sake. However, it is possible to trace a shift in the appearance of the Shaker building from complete simplicity to a kind of stripped Classicism. The proportions and the sense of scale imparted to buildings such as the 56-room dwelling house at Canterbury, built in 1793, shows that even some of the earliest Shaker architecture could draw on Classical principles. The use of a pedimented porch supported by columns, placed squarely in the middle of the symmetrical façade, gives something of the air of an English country house, and a cupola surmounts the pitched roof.

Most early Shaker meeting houses were of clapboard clothing a timber frame, and drew on an unassuming vernacular vocabulary for their form. Later dwelling houses used an architectural language which had its roots firmly in the middle-class taste of the private builder. The Shaker brethren who built these fine houses were not in any way compromised in terms of their faith or their dedication to the maintenance of the Shaker way. But as the Shaker sect grew and had increasing contact with the outside world, some influence was inevitably absorbed. This is what makes Shaker architecture, for all its intriguing contradictions, quintessentially American in character.

In the hands of its 'mechanics', the architecture of the Shakers was at once reminiscent of Scandinavian vernacular buildings and characterized by Georgian propriety and symmetry and the 'new tradition' of architecture conditioned by the materials and climate of the north-eastern seaboard of America.

The Great Stone Dwelling at Enfield, New Hampshire was built in granite in 1837 from blocks quarried from Shaker land. It stands six storeys high, with the upper two storeys used as attic space. The pitched roof is surmounted by a cupola of a slightly decorative nature which housed a bell for the summoning of brethren and sisters to worship and meals. It is an impressive building

**RIGHT** *Meeting House and Dwelling House, Canterbury, New Hampshire, 1792–3. As with all early meeting houses, the example at Canterbury follows the original pattern set at New Lebanon.*

**RIGHT** *Meeting House at Canterbury, New Hampshire. Note the clapboard covering, sash windows and sense of proportion which is characteristic of most Shaker architecture. The bell tower or cupola also became a familiar feature on later dwelling houses in many Shaker communities.*

and has a simple grandeur that is Classical in spirit. But Shaker buildings were also shaped by the ritualistic, highly organized life which was to be lived within their walls. Their design was considerably determined by the sect's devotion to neatness, cleanliness, plainness, celibacy, sexual segregation and communality. Most of the early meeting and dwelling houses have two front doors, one for the sisters and one for the brethren. In this way the opportunities for contact and social intercourse between the sexes was kept to a minimum and could be confined to the times specifically set aside for 'union meetings'. This division in the entrances to a building was often extended through to the stairwells. Communality would be enforced through the design of the retiring rooms, which usually accommodated four or five brethren or sisters who would share responsibility for domestic tasks.

The greatest communal bond was perhaps achieved through the extraordinary system of worship practised by the Shakers involving well-disciplined, shuffling dance steps. Sufficient uninterrupted space had to be designed into the meeting and dwelling houses to allow for the execution of, for example, a 'square order shuffle' by close on 100 Believers. The need for these large spaces, unbroken by supporting pillars, produced a range of architectural solutions from something akin to medieval hammer-beamed roofs to barn technology: they are remarkable for their high standard of workmanship, their inventiveness, and their exclusively wooden constructions.

The meeting house at New Lebanon, New York, constructed in 1824, is perhaps the finest example of Shaker ingenuity in wooden architecture. It is certainly the largest meeting house ever constructed. In 1824, the popularity of Shakerism was nearing its zenith and the new meeting house was constructed to replace the old one, which had served as the prototype for meeting houses in Shaker communities all over the country. The 65ft × 80ft (19.5m x 24m) space on the first floor of the building is uninterrupted by

**BELOW** *Centre Family Dwelling, South Union, Kentucky, 1824. The double staircase ensured that bretheren and sisters would move from the dining room to their retiring rooms in separate parts of the house with no opportunity to converse. The adherence to sexual segregation determined the design of many Shaker buildings.*

supporting pillars and could accommodate 500 worshipful Believers and up to 1,000 spectators. The construction of such a large, light and airy space was achieved through the use of a barrel roof, tied together with a web of timber-framing from which the ceiling of the meeting room is suspended.

The meeting house at Canterbury, New Hampshire, built in 1792, conforms to the model of the earlier New Lebanon meeting house. Shakers believed that the ministry at New Lebanon was divinely inspired and that, as the fountainhead of Shakerism, the Church Family there received the ultimate messages about the way the Shaker world should be built. There is a further explanation of the persistence of the New Lebanon design: many of the buildings erected during the busiest phase of Shaker expansion and consolidation between 1792 and the mid-19th century were the work of the same group of Shaker 'engineers' or 'mechanics' who would travel around visiting each community as and when it needed their skills. Thus the names of Moses Johnson (1752–1842) and Elder William Deming (1779–1849) appear with regularity in the records of Shaker architecture.

Moses Johnson held tenure as the master builder at the New Lebanon community for many years, and it was he who was responsible for the Canterbury meeting house. It is timber-framed and has a gambrel roof, so-called for the resemblance of its profile to the hind leg of a horse, with dormer windows in the

**LEFT** *The Meeting House at New Lebanon, New York, 1824. This extraordinary structure represented a departure for the Shakers. Built to replace what had been seen as the perfect model for the Shaker meeting house, the need for space engendered a radical new design.*

ABOVE *The interior of the Round Stone Barn, Hancock, Massachusetts, 1826. A complex web of timber framing demonstrates the skill of the Shaker engineers in working with their most readily available material.*

lower slope. This shape of roof was well adapted to the New England climate, with its high rainfall and heavy snows. The meeting house stands on the edge of the wood from which the materials for its construction came. The walls are white-painted clapboard. For many years there was a convention among the Shakers that the meeting house should be the only building in the community painted white. This reflected the fact that white paint was more expensive than any other colour. However, advances of the chemical industry in the young United States reduced the price differential and the practice of painting paticular types of building particular colours diminished, although work buildings continued to be coloured either in red, tan or yellow. A further decline in the observance of the painting rules took place as the Shakers spread across America, encountering different building materials and turning to more permanent forms of construction. Always striving to be in harmony with their surroundings and to utilize whichever gifts God placed in their way, the Shakers were bound to advance the techniques of building as the opportunity arose.

The buildings of the Church Family at Hancock, Massachusetts provide a good example of the way in which a community expressed its material and cultural progress through building. The first building, erected in 1790, is the small meeting house which characteristically is based on the original at New Lebanon; it is white-painted, has a gambrel roof and provided the accommodation for the elders and eldresses. In about 1800, significantly, the laundry and machine shop were housed under one roof in a large wooden building – a three-storey structure with a pitched roof. In this building were carried out chair – and clockmaking, seed packaging and so on, all of which formed the basis for the financial security which would allow for the construction in 1826 of the famous Round Stone Barn, designed by the Shaker mechanic Daniel Goodrich (1765–1835). Although this is by no means the only round barn in the north-eastern states it is nonetheless unique in the world of the Shakers. The principal architectural form is derived from Scandinavian tradition, adopted and adapted by the Shakers for their own needs. This community was obviously building for future generations when the plans for the barn were laid. It had provision for 50 head of cattle and was designed like a great machine for the storage of livestock and hay in the winter months. Measuring 270ft (81m) in circumference the barn has three floors, each of which is accessible from the ground floor by means of ramps. The top floor is designated for hay wagons, which were driven in and unloaded into the central well while they circled on the wooden balcony. In this fashion up to 10 hay

RIGHT *The Round Stone Barn, Hancock Massachusetts, 1826. The form of this barn is based on a type commonly found in Scandinavia; the Shakers were adept at appropriating the vernacular for their own needs.*

wains could be unloaded at one time. The second floor was reserved for the cattle stalls which were ranged against the outside
wall. The ground floor had provision for the collection and
removal of the cattle dung which would then be ploughed back
into the soil in the spring. In spite of an ingenious vented central
shaft designed to keep air circulating through the hay to prevent
the spontaneous combustion of accumulations of hay dust, the
barn caught fire in 1864, but the stone walls survived, allowing
the still-pragmatic Shakers to build to an even grander design. A
new roof in the form of a clerestory was built on top of a new
addition to the already imposing building. This allowed for the
admission of more daylight to the upper storeys. The addition of a
hexagonal turret surmounted by a windvane was the final touch.

The next building to appear in Hancock was a further indication

**RIGHT** *The Hancock
community. The scale of
the development of the
Hancock community
was by no means
unusual for Shaker
groups, although
Hancock proved to be
one of the sect's most
vital communities. The
last buildings were
being erected here as late
as 1939.*

of the prosperity and security which the Church Family had found. Designed by elder William Deming (1779–1849) the Church Family Dwelling is a magnificent brick-built structure of six storeys which, when fully occupied and in use, could house nearly 100 Shaker brethren and sisters. It features a grey slate roof with a cupola housing a bell at the southern end. There is a two-storey attic for storage; the fourth and third floors house retiring rooms; the second floor has the public rooms, dining rooms and family meeting room, and kitchens and more storage space are located in the semi-basement or first floor. The dining room was originally distinctive for the dividing walls which could be lowered into the centre of the room by a system of pulleys. Separate rooms for brethren and sisters could thus be created, with a hallway in between for absolute privacy. The bare and unadorned red-brick

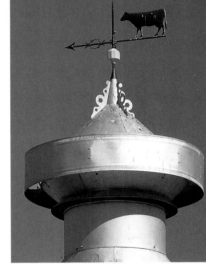

**ABOVE** *The weathervane, Round Stone Barn, Hancock, Massachusetts.*

**LEFT** *The Horse Barn at Hancock. In early Shaker communities, only the Meeting House could be painted white. Later, as white paint became less hard to come by, it became more common to paint other buildings in the colour which had once symbolized purity to the Shakers.*

exterior of this dwelling is impressive for its scale, symmetry and solidity. It represents much of what is best in Shaker architecture. William Deming himself described the building of the dwelling house in 1832:

> WE COMMENCED OUR BUILDING AND IN TEN WEEKS FROM THE PLACING OF THE FIRST STONE IN THE CELLAR THE HOUSE WAS NEATLY LAID UP AND THE ROOF PUT ON. THE WORK IS ALL WELL DONE. THERE IS NONE TO EXCELL IT IN THIS COUNTRY . . . WE HAVE FOUND ALL THE MATERIALS OURSELVES SUCH AS SAND, LIME, STONE, ETC. WITH ALL THE TIMBER EXCEPT THE FLOORING. WE HAVE MADE ALL THE WINDOWS, DOORS, CUPBOARDS AND DRAWERS . . . WITH ALL THIS AND A GREAT DEAL MORE THAT WE HAVE DONE OURSELVES THE OUT EXPENSES ARE ABOUT $6,000.

Behind the construction of such a large dwelling lay Mother Ann's advice, 'Put your hands to work and your hearts to God and a blessing will attend you'. Faith in the ultimate success of the Shaker experiment was high. The expectation of greater things from the investment in spiritually inspired labour was the spur to advancement. In 1830, $8,000 was no mean sum of money: the investment of such a sum speaks clearly of the success and confidence of the Shaker movement at this time.

In 1840 a tan house was built for the processing and working of leather for saddles, shoes, belts and boots. In 1878 a brick-built poultry house was added. It is a curiuous anomaly in terms of the Shaker approach to architecture, considering that wood would have sufficed. It at first appears to be symmetrical in elevation, with four small windows on the first storey; however, the larger

**ABOVE** *Wooden outbuildings at Hancock, Massachusetts.*

**LEFT** *The Tannery at New (Mount) Lebanon, built in the early 19th century. Shakers diversified their manufacturing interests, and the communities grew, thanks to burgeoning trade with the outside world. In spite of it being a working building, the Tannery exhibits all the traits common to Shaker architecture in its use of materials, proportion and general design.*

windows on the ground floor are arranged either side of the entrance with five on one side and six on the other, a device which unbalances an otherwise plain and typically utilitarian Shaker building. The last building on the Hancock site was as late as 1939, with the addition of some dairy buildings next to the Round Barn.

The scale of the development in Hancock was by no means unique. The barn at the New Lebanon community was also huge, measuring 296ft × 50ft (88.8m × 18m), but was completely destroyed by fire in 1972. Built five storeys high with a slate roof, it was designed for use by the North Family. The barn was built into a hillside, so that access was available to all three floors from ground level. Its length was designed to accommodate ten hay wagons in the event of a sudden rainstorm, while the width was based on the space needed for the turning of a hay wagon and team inside the barn.

Further south, in Kentucky, two flourishing Shaker communities, at South Union and Pleasant Valley, expressed their new-found

**BELOW** *The Shaker community at Pleasant Hill, Kentucky.*

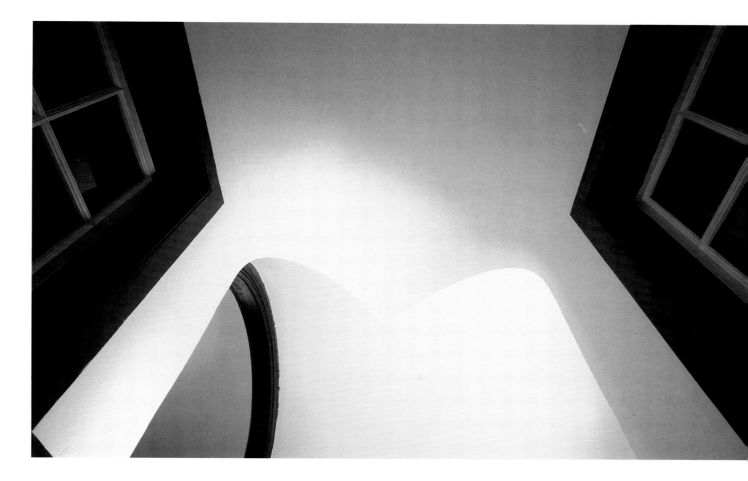

ABOVE *The hall leading to the Meeting Room, Pleasant Hill, Kentucky. The rooms in the buildings at Pleasant Hill and other sites in Kentucky generally exhibited higher ceilings than their northern counterparts as a concession to the warmer climate. The recurrent use of curvilinear forms in Kentucky Shaker architecture is also a unique feature.*

stability in the buildings the brethren constructed for themselves and their sisters. The Center Family Dwelling at Pleasant Valley, begun in 1824, is perhaps the best example of the effect of the 'colonial' styles on what was supposed to be the unadorned aesthetic of Shaker architecture. It had a stripped Georgian façade, augmented by the addition of European-type external shutters. The front of the building is completely symmetrical and includes the usual double front doors for the admission of sisters and brethren. The house is surrounded by the customary picket fence, and the entire building is of Kentucky limestone. A curious feature of this building is a small gazebo at one end of the roof giving access to a viewing platform. The gazebo has a Gothic window which seems to be very much at odds with the Shakers' affirmed disavowal of style for style's sake. The platform is surrounded by a Romanesque balustrade. The general appearance is that of a whimsical addition to what is otherwise a solid and well-proportioned Shaker dwelling of more than 40 rooms. In its heyday this house, like that at Hancock, would have provided accommodation for close on 100 Believers, giving some indication of

**RIGHT** *The Brick Dwelling House, Hancock, New Hampshire.*

the strength of the Shaker movement in the area of the Kentucky Revival.

The Kentucky Pleasant Valley community also houses one of the finest pieces of interior architecture to be found in Shakerdom. In the Trustees' Office, built in 1831, there is a highly impressive double spiral staircase. It is a twin helix of startling and graceful proportions, winding up through the building. The workmanship of the staircase is outstanding. There are delicate ogee mouldings around each tread, with the risers left plain. The sinuous banister rail is steamed from sections of an unidentified stained hardwood, while the banisters themselves are of the simplest and unadorned inch-square hickory, also lightly stained. Answering the banister rail in the gently curving wall opposite is another semi-circular rail. The impression given by the whole is one of lightness and deftness in execution and sturdiness and strength in use.

The Trustees' Office was the place where visitors from 'the world' were billeted when they came to trade with the Shakers. Clearly such an impressively designed and built structure would have left its mark on the strangers who stayed there, no doubt arousing in them a sense of respect for these people who could build so well. Clearly, even for a sect as self-effacing as the Shakers, public statements of worthiness and honorability were often made in the form of buildings.

In South Union, Kentucky, there is a further example of the success of the Shakers in the dwelling house built for the Centre Family in 1822–33 under the guidance of Benjamin Youngs (1774–1855), with Robert Johns (1795–1863) the head carpenter. This brick-built dwelling is unusual, in that it does not use the device of the double entrance but instead has two sets of steps leading up to a single panelled door. Although the Shaker brethren and sisters had to use the same door, the likelihood is that they would have entered at different times to maintain the segregation of the sexes upon which a great deal of Shaker order depended. This dwelling is completely symmetrical in elevation and is as plain and unadorned a piece of architecture as the most strict Shaker could wish to have seen. The semi-basement, which is faced in limestone on the outer walls, is home to the bakery, the kitchen, six store rooms and a dining room. On the first floor can

**BELOW** *The interior of the Ministry Shop, Sabbathday Lake, Maine.*

**ABOVE** *Retiring room, Sabbathday Lake, Maine. The colour scheme of deep blue/green woodwork and white walls was common to both retiring rooms and meeting halls in Shaker communities all over the American continent.*

be found the large family meeting room and ten retiring rooms. The second floor houses ten more retiring rooms, and the top floor yet more, as well as a spacious attic lit by dormer windows.

Most houses in New England were planned traditionally, around the central core of the fireplace and chimney stack. Shaker dwelling houses often departed from this plan. In a house designed to accommodate over 100 people, a large meeting hall, kitchens and other amenities, a plan centred on a single chimney stack would prove impractical. Instead, the Shakers used enclosed stoves feeding into a common chimney stack via stove pipes. Bitter experience had taught that closed stoves provided the safest method of heating in timber dwellings and they were also economical and efficient.

Shaker interiors were always characterized by provision for the pursuit of fastidious cleanliness, together with a degree of lightness and grace which was an accident of taste created by the rejection of worldly superfluity and the maintenance of a 'good eye' by the Shaker craftsmen.

The Shaker interior, for all its simplicity, was not devoid of colour. Far from being completely against ornamentation, the Shakers were theosophic in their use of stains, washes and varnishes in the meeting houses, retiring rooms and storage spaces of their buildings. The idea that the Shaker chair was made by someone capable of believing that an angel would sit on it is not new, but it does illustrate the Shakers' approach to the decoration of their interior spaces. The perception of their own living spaces as the earthly manifestation of a heavenly archetype had come as divine inspiration to the Shakers. Paradise to the Believers was clean, simple and decorated with the muted colours of blues and greens, some indoor plants and the play of sunlight on floors polished by many hours of worshipful dances in specially made soft shoes. The meeting room used by the Centre Family at Pleasant Hill, Kentucky is one such example. The walls are plaster-covered and there is a high, arched roof reminiscent of the one in the meeting house at New Lebanon. The floor is neatly laid in the customary pine and it is well-polished. Wainscoting rises to just below 3ft (90cm) up the walls; it is stained a deep blue-green and matches the window frames and the peg rail which extends around the walls. The room is unusual in that there is an arched 'Gothic' paned window above the door. The meeting house is oriented so that sunlight comes through the large windows all day long. The effect is as pleasing as any Shaker room could be, and illustrates the 'divinely inspired' approach to interior decoration which was so characteristic of Shaker architecture in all its manifestations.

**RIGHT** *Shaker interior with dormer window set into the gambrel roof. The sewing stand contains pincushions and other needleworking paraphanalia, and a nest of nice boxes and winding device stand on the window sill.*

# 4

## THE SPREAD OF
## THE SHAKERS
## ACROSS AMERICA

**LEFT** *The Meeting
House, Canterbury, New
Hampshire, 1792.*

**ABOVE** *Shaker camp. In the early days of the sect, Shakers from around the country used to gather in camps such as this for prayer and worship.*

In many ways the spread of Shakerism is closely linked to the growth of the nation we now know as America. When the Constitution was ratified in 1791, two of the amendments canonized the principle of freedom of speech and the notion that all men are born equal. These two fundaments of the American way are closely allied to the Shaker philosophy. At the same time, the Revolution and the Declaration of Independence paved the way for the opening up of the continent to the newly American inhabitants of the original 13 states. In 1803, with the Louisiana Purchase, the boundaries of the Union were extended to the Rocky Mountains and the Hispanic and French interests in the New World were bought from Napoleon for the princely sum of $15 million. 'The greatest real estate deal in history' also meant that settlers could now move into a vast continental hinterland in search of the mythical promised land. With this one historic purchase the nation was doubled in size and the potential for development was increased proportionately. The Shakers could not have found themselves in a better place at a better time, and the rapid expansion and consolidation of their faith is a testament to this happy coincidence.

The first Shaker societies were founded on the eastern seaboard in New York State by Ann Lee and her followers. The first tract of land was probably paid for by John Hockley, one of the members of the original party that sailed from England in 1774. It was he who had raised the money for the passage to America in the first place, but although he was obviously important to the birth of the Shaker movement little else is known of him. From these beginnings in the woods of New York State near the town of Albany, where the Shaker settlers had made a clearing and built log cabins in which to live, there grew what would be described as the foremost communistic society in the US.

A major factor in the geographic spread of the Shaker movement in the early 19th century was the so-called Kentucky Revival that began in 1801. This was according to Charles Nordhoff, 'a remarkable religious excitement lasting several years and attended with extraordinary and in some cases horrible physical demonstrations. Camp meetings were held in different counties to which people flocked in their thousands; and here men and women and even small children fell down in convulsions, foamed at the mouth and uttered loud cries.' This religious fervour swept through the towns in the Bluegrass state of Kentucky, and enabled the Shakers to bring their Adventist message to willing ears.

In 1807 a Shaker chair maker, Richard McNemar, published his account of the events surrounding the Kentucky Revival in a

**RIGHT** *Tape loom from c1839, attributed to carpenters at New Lebanon, New York, and now part of the Sherman collection.*

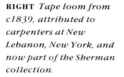

**ABOVE** *Even the most utilitarian of objects were beautifully finished by the Shaker craftsmen, as this wooden shovel shows.*

**LEFT** *The growth of Shakerism required precise construction of the new communities, creating consistency and a sense of unity. The correctness of Shaker building design came to rest on the skilfull use of instruments like these.*

pamphlet entitled *The Kentucky Revival or a Short History of the late extraordinary outpouring of the spirit in the Western States of America*. Parts of the account make unbelievable and harrowing reading but, as more than one commentator has remarked, there is no reason for doubting the testimony of this Shaker who was a witness to the extraordinary scenes. During the revival great crowds would flock to makeshift campsites to experience the effect of the 'outpouring of the spirit', described by McNemar thus: 'At first they were taken with an inward throbbing of the heart; then weeping and trembling; from that to apparent crying out in the agony of the soul; falling down and swooning away until every appearance of animal life would be suspended and the person would appear to be in a trance.' This individual experience would sometimes be multiplied, as at Cabin Creek in May 1801, where 'a great number fell on the third night and to prevent being trodden underfoot by the multitude they were collected together and laid out in order in two squares of the meeting house, which like so many dead corpses covered a considerable part of the floor.' The experience of such religious fervour extended to many different people in a kind of mass hysteria, as McNemar further comments: 'no sex or color, class or description were exempted from the pervading influence of the spirit from the age of eight months to 60 years.'

Hearing of the excitement in the counties of Kentucky, the Shakers at New Lebanon despatched three men on a journey to open the testimony to those in the state who were willing to receive it. The convulsions and collapsing of these congregations bore a remarkable similarity to the Shakers' 'coming under operations', and no doubt the delegation sent to Kentucky was aware of this. The opening of the testimony in Kentucky was therefore a divinely inspired but nonetheless shrewd move. Benjamin Youngs, John Meacham and Issacher Bates set off from New Lebanon on New Year's Day, 1805, and travelled 1,000 miles on foot; the net result of their journey was that two settlements were opened in Ohio, two in Kentucky and one in Indiana, although this last settlement was short-lived and eventually also moved to Kentucky. In much the same way some 20 years earlier Mother Ann herself had gone out from Watervliet and spent the years from 1781 to 1783 on the road preaching the Shaker faith to all who would listen. No doubt she had been encouraged by the effects of her preaching from between the bars of a prison cell where she had been imprisoned with some of her followers in 1780; upon her release by Governor George Clinton she found that she had acquired a reputation, which no doubt helped in her spreading of the Shaker doctrine.

**ABOVE** *The spread of the Shakers across America resulted in the consolidation of a lucrative seed trade. Shaker seeds became famous for their reliability and consistent quality.*

The settlements which grew up during the ensuing 107 years covered the continent from Watervliet in the east to Kentucky in the west and even Florida in the south. Economically and in terms of population, the communities reached their peak in the early part of the 19th century. By the mid-19th century most of them were declining in population but economically were still reasonably secure. Their initial need to establish themselves on the frontiers of the new America had meant that the provisions they had made for economic security were often more than adequate. Once industries and farms were up and running on their strict Shaker lines, they continued, and although some societies lost money by going against the maxim that they 'should owe no man anything', most of the societies were prosperous. Those that were not weř usually under the protection of a larger society and so absolute ruin was avoided.

In the 1850s Shaker populations were in decline but the industries and settlements were at their peak. Most of the major building and consolidation of settlements had occurred in the first 40 years of the century. So, when Charles Nordhoff undertook his survey of the Shakers at that time, his findings illustrate the Shaker world, its interests, its industries and its people more or less in their prime, on the eve of the American Civil War.

The Shaker settlement at Alfred, Maine was one of the earliest, established in 1793. Covering 1,100 acres, it lies in the hills in York County, and has readily available water power to drive its machinery. The community was gathered to order in 1794 and consisted of two Families. Industries that formed the backbone of the community's economy were the raising of garden seeds, the manufacture of brooms, wire sieves and dry measures. There was a tannery to provide for the leather needs of the community and a grist mill which were owned by the Shakers but leased to commercial companies outside the Shaker world. The women were generally engaged in the running of the dwellings and the making of fans and baskets, which would be sold at nearby seaside towns during the summer. It is generally accepted that the first circular saw ever made in the USA was invented by a Shaker at Alfred, Maine.

**BELOW** *Basket-making was a staple earner in many of the growing communities, providing much needed revenue as well as utility objects for use in Shaker kitchens, gardens and on the farms.*

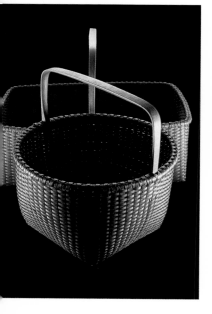

**RIGHT** *A barn at Pleasant Hill, Kentucky.*

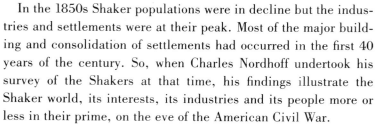

The community at New Gloucester, Maine was established in 1794, and originally included farmers, merchants, printers, wool weavers and some mechanics. At its peak it consisted of two Families, the Gathering and the Church, and was a successful settlement with 150 members. With 2,000 acres and boasting a sawmill, grist mill and a machine shop, the Shakers of New Gloucester also raised seed and made brooms, dry measures and wire sieves. They were also responsible for a type of spinning wheel, now endemic to Maine and New Hampshire, that is used to make stocking yarn. The greatest source of income for this community came from the manufacture of oak staves for the hogs-heads that were used to transport molasses. Hewitt Chandler, a mechanic at this settlement, developed a method for the bending of barrel staves before they were set into the cask, so making the

**LEFT** *A hinged box for carrying samples of Shaker dried herbs, the basis of yet another Shaker trade.*

LEFT *The Shakers in many communities were adept at brush- and broom-making. Products of the Shaker manufacturies were generally highly regarded for their resilience and effectiveness.*

task of coopering easier and more efficient. He was also the inventor of a mowing machine, manufactured at New Gloucester and sold to 'the world' for many years. In 1858, the Shaker sisters of New Gloucester capitalized on their culinary skills by making and selling $1,000 worth of pickles!

The Shakers at Canterbury, New Hampshire were the proprietors of what was one of the largest and most successful communities. Three families lived on 3,000 acres in a community which was first established in 1792. As well as the 3,000 acres of homestead, they also owned a sheep farm in western New York State with 800 head of sheep grazing upon it. In terms of manufacture, this community was perhaps the closest the Shakers ever came to heavy industry. They were the inventors and makers of large washing machines and mangles which were marketed to hotels in Boston and New York. The community held the patents on these machines and so they were a reliable source of income. The Canterbury Families enjoyed the benefit of a steam laundry on site to ensure the neat appearance of the brethren and sisters (numbering 300 at their peak) who laboured in the various indus-

BELOW *A Shaker print shop. Under the direction of Elder William Deming, the Shakers at New (later Mount) Lebanon produced and distributed several tracts as well as a regular newspaper,* The Shaker.

tries that kept this community in the style to which it had become accustomed. Apart from the usual making of brooms, fancies for tourists and the running of a sawmill, the Shakers here also sold hay, wove woollen cloth and made sarsaparilla syrup and checkerberry oil. They also knitted vast quantities of woollen socks on knitting machines. A tannery turned out leather for shoes, boots, saddles, and whips, while other shops manufactured mortars and sieves. The community also owned an hotel near the railway track after the coming of the steam locomotive in the 1830s. It was an imposing red-brick building for the use of visitors to the nearby sulphurous spring and the Shakers themselves and the guests at the hotel were bound by Shaker rules during their stay. A sign in the reception area stated: 'Married persons tarrying with us overnight are respectfully notified that each sex operate separate sleeping apartments while they remain.'

The community at Enfield, New Hampshire was gathered to order in 1793, and is most famous for the large granite-built dwellings which occupy parts of the 3,000-acre site. The Church Family Dwelling measures 100ft × 60ft (30m × 18m) and stand six storeys high. At its peak the population was 330, divided between 3 Families. The Church Family enjoyed the benefits of a water-powered laundry with a centrifugal drier instead of the more usual system of mangles and wringers. The Shakers of Enfield were the first to make a business out of the raising and selling of garden seeds, but like other Shaker communities they were involved in many different enterprises. They manufactured buckets, tubs and dry measures, and dried herbs, roots and vegetables for medicines. It was from Enfield that patent medicines, such as the 'Shaker Anodyne' and the 'Fluid Valerian Extract', originated. While knitting machines produced flannel shirts, drawers and socks, the sisters sewed shirts which would be sold in Boston. The sisters were also involved in the production of maple syrup in the spring and apple sauce in the winter, as well as bread, pies and other provisions for sale in the local villages. The community owned and leased to worldly interests a grist mill and a woollen mill. Against the workaday image of many Shaker inventions, one brother in the Enfield community actually invented and patented a pocket stereoscope, which sadly never caught on.

In contrast to the almost industrial bent of many Shaker communities, some relied on their agronomical skills to make a living. Such were the brethren and sisters at the community at Enfield, New Hampshire. Founded in 1792 on 3,300 acres of land, this community existed as four Families, and at its peak had 200 members. When the coming of automation and factory practices

made the closure of the original lead-pipe factory imminent, these Shakers turned to cattle-breeding as the staple of their income. They also sold hay, enabling them in turn to buy Indian corn, which could then be dried and stored.

In Massachusetts, the Harvard community, founded in 1793 on 1,800 acres, relied on farming for its self-sufficiency, owning two farms outside the main settlement, in Michigan and Massachusetts. Populated at its peak by four Families totalling 200 members, the Harvard community was one that, although it made brooms, pressed herbs and ran a seed nursery, stayed closest to the original Shaker ideal of self-sufficiency without large profit. The original philosophy that governed Shaker work was to have just enough to get by, and some put by for harder times should they arise. Clearly, some communities exceeded this simple dictum. One such was the community at Shirley, Massachusetts which, although it stood on 2,000 acres, also owned several outlying farms. At its peak, the 150 inhabitants of the community were able to survive by making and selling five to six tons (5,000–6,000kg) of apple sauce per year along with fruit preserves, jellies, pickles, dried corn, maple sugar and the ubiquitous brooms.

The Shakers at New Lebanon, New York (renamed Mount Lebanon in the 1860s), founded in 1787, were viewed as the parent community of the whole movement. At one time 5–600 Shakers lived in some seven Family groups on 3,000 acres of New York State land. The Shakers at New Lebanon were more than solvent, owning farms in several other states and taking as payment for the leases half of the crops produced. Income from these land interests was supplemented by trade in seeds, brooms, herbs and herb extracts, dried sweet corn, chairs, mops, woven mats, fans and dusters. The New Lebanon Shakers were also extensive sheep keepers.

**LEFT** *Machine House at Hancock, Massachusetts.*

At Watervliet, New York, the brethren and sisters speculated heavily in land. As well as the 4,500 acres upon which their settlement was built, they owned a further 32,000 acres in other states upon which they farmed sheep. Although theirs was not the biggest settlement, the Watervliet Shakers had at the time 350 members in four Families. Other money-earning ventures included a short-lived tannery, the cultivation of both broom- and sweetcorn, a cannery for fruit and vegetables, the raising and selling of garden seeds, and shoe, carpet, clothing and furniture manufactories. This community employed up to 75 outside labourers at any one time. In the eyes of some Shaker elders this kind of expansion and interaction with the world diluted the purity of the sect. Nevertheless, economic necessity demanded the successful running of these businesses for the good of Shakerism as a whole, and at times it was fine balancing act between the interests of the world and the interests of what was supposed to be an exclusive society. The Watervliet community needed to maintain its interest in worldly affairs to enable it to discharge its responsibilities. For example, it was the Watervliet community that had charge of the welfare of the only entirely black Family in Shakerdom. These were 12 women, freed slaves, who had joined the sect. They differed from other Shaker Families in that they lived apart from an established community in Philadelphia and worked as maids in private houses, returning to the Shaker dwelling at the end of each working day. Because they had no means of self-support apart from their wages as servants, they were placed under the aegis of the Watervliet community who made sure that they did not go in need of any of the staples of life.

The establishment of a Shaker community often involved a fortuitous meeting with a local farmer who happened to be in the market for salvation. The Shaker rule requiring newly recruited members to surrender all their property to the general ownership

**ABOVE** *The Shakers endeavoured to ensure their survival by introducing elements of self sufficiency into their lives. The growing and harvesting of apples meant that apple sauce became part of the Shaker staple diet. It was often eaten for supper with milk and bread.*

**LEFT** *The cottage industries of the Shakers ranged from pharmacy to wool spinning. The spinning wheel here is typical of many that would have been used by the Shaker sisters.*

of the sect thus meant that new communities often had a good, solid base from which to start. One such settlement was started in Ohio as a result of the Shaker interest in the Kentucky Revival. The three witnesses who had been sent out from New Lebanon were met on the way by Malchus Worley who, convinced by their testimony, became a Believer and donated his land to the Shaker cause. The community of Union Village was born in 1805 on the 4,500 acres formally owned by Worley: it subsequently grew into a community of four Families and 600 inhabitants. The community at South Union, Kentucky was established in 1809, also at the time of the Kentucky Revival. Its 6,000 acres accommodated 350 people in four Families. Here, with the outlawing of slavery after the Civil War, the ranks of the Shakers were swollen by repenting slave owners who found themselves living side-by-side with their erstwhile slaves and having to declare brotherhood, sisterhood and egality with men and women they had formerly owned. The Shaker way of life must have been a powerful draw indeed for this to have occurred amongst the white people of the pro-slavery South and their black brothers and sisters. The Shakers at South Union indulged in the usual trades, as well as raising

**ABOVE** *A wide Shaker broom. This type of broom would have been used for sweeping the broad expanses of wooden floor found in all dwelling houses.*

**RIGHT** *Farm buildings at Hancock, Massachusetts.*

cattle, sheep and chickens, running extensive orchards and cultivating crops of wheat, rye and oats. A hotel and shop in the nearby town also brought in much-needed revenue.

It was certainly true of many Shaker communities that economic success bred complacency. Once well-established in a region, most Shaker communities became wealthy enough not to have to bother with the recruiting of new members or with the maintenance of the sect itself, preferring instead a *laisser faire* attitude. The circumstances of history – the birth of a new nation with ideas that seemed to correspond to the Shakers' own, and the need among many struggling new Americans for the order, physical and spiritual, that the Shaker experiment represented – allowed the Shakers their initial success. But time did not stand still, and America was changing. In all, some 19 Shaker communities came into existence during a 100-year period, with several short-lived so-called 'out Families' swelling the numbers further. At their peak in the early 19th century there were around 6,000 Shakers in the USA; now there are less than 12.

**ABOVE** *Early colonial life is recreated at Sturbridge colonial village, Massachusetts.*

**LEFT** *Shaker buildings at Hancock, Massachusetts.*

**DISTRIBUTION AND SPREAD OF THE SHAKER POPULATION ACROSS THE UNITED STATES**

KEY
- SHAKER COMMUNITIES
- CITIES
— STATE LINES
▲ EXISTING COMMUNITY
△ RESTORED BUILDINGS OR MUSEUM
◇ FORMER COMMUNITY

| NOS: | COMMUNITIES | | FOUNDING DATE |
|---|---|---|---|
| 1 | New Lebanon, New York (later Mount Lebanon) | △ | 1787 |
| 2 | Watervliet, New York | △ | 1787 |
| 3 | Enfield, Connecticut | ◇ | 1790 |
| 4 | Hancock, Massachusetts | △ | 1790 |
| 5 | Harvard, Massachusetts | ◇ | 1791 |
| 6 | Canterbury, New Hampshire | ▲ | 1792 |
| 7 | Tyringham, Massachusetts | ◇ | 1792 |
| 8 | Alfred, Maine | ◇ | 1793 |
| 9 | Enfield, New Hampshire | △ | 1793 |
| 10 | Shirley, Massachusetts | ◇ | 1793 |
| 11 | New Gloucester, Maine (later Sabbathday Lake) | ▲ | 1794 |
| 12 | Pleasant Hill, Kentucky | △ | 1806 |
| 13 | Union Village, Ohio | ◇ | 1806 |
| 14 | Watervliet, Ohio | ◇ | 1806 |
| 15 | South Union, Kentucky | △ | 1807 |
| 16 | Gorham, Maine | ◇ | 1808 |
| 17 | West Union, Indiana | ◇ | 1810 |
| 18 | Savoy, Massachusetts | ◇ | 1817 |
| 19 | North Union, Ohio | ◇ | 1822 |
| 20 | Whitewater, Ohio | ◇ | 1824 |
| 21 | Groveland, New York | ◇ | 1836 |
| 22 | Sodus Bay, New York | ◇ | 1826 |
| 23 | Narcoossee, Florida | ◇ | 1896 |
| 24 | White Oak, Georgia | ◇ | 1898 |

# 5

# SHAKER LIFE, WORK AND WORSHIP

**LEFT** *Certain Shaker industries such as small-scale sheep farming are continued today in the much-reduced communities.*

The *Summary View*, published in the early 19th century as a resumé for both the Shakers themselves and the outside world of the way in which the order should be lived, stated that 'all members are equally holden according to their several abilities to maintain one united interest and therefore all labour with their hands in some useful occupation for the mutual comfort and benefit of themselves and each other and for the general good of the family or society to which they belong.' To that end, ministers, elders, eldresses, deacons and deaconesses were all expected to engage in some useful work for the benefit of the community to which they belonged. Shaker life, work and worship formed an unassailable trinity, with each of the constituent parts inextricably bound up with the others. Life, to a Shaker, was supposed to consist of

**LEFT** *Eldress Gertrude, a surviving Shaker sister knitting on the porch at Canterbury, New Hampshire.*

**ABOVE** *The Cobbler's Room, Bretherens' Shop, Hancock, Massachusetts. The leather produced by the Shaker tanneries was most often worked in the Shakers' own cobblers shops, producing shoes for the bretheren and sisters of the community.*

labour for the betterment of the soul, and thereby for the perfection of existence on earth. Worship was a part of this life, and was seen as a further source of labour by which the brethren and sisters could advance toward their ideal. The Believer, therefore, was bound up in a cyclical existence in which, theologically and philosophically, no divisions existed between the three spheres.

The primary division experienced by the Shaker brother and sister was between the sexes, for, as we have seen, celibacy was one of the fundamental orders that governed life in a Shaker dwelling house. This was a dictate enshrined in the Millennial Laws, and was observed at all times by brethren and sisters alike. The only opportunity for intercourse of any kind came with the union meetings, which was held in the retiring rooms of brethren and would last for one hour, perhaps three times a week. During this time the Shakers would be allowed to converse simply on any subject connected with their life and work in the Shaker community. The union meetings were described by Harvey Elkins of Enfield, New Hampshire, in his *Fifteen Years in the Senior Order of Shakers'*, first published in 1853:

**RIGHT** *The Meeting House at New (Mount) Lebanon, 1824. This Meeting House was specifically designed to house up to 1,000 spectators from the outside world, a good indication of the level of interest generated by Shakerism during the early part of the 19th century.*

FOR THE UNION MEETINGS THE BRETHREN REMAIN IN THEIR ROOMS AND THE SISTERS, SIX, EIGHT OR TEN IN NUMBER, ENTER AND SIT IN A RANK OPPOSITE TO THAT OF THE BRETHREN'S, AND CONVERSE SIMPLY OFTEN FACETIOUSLY, BUT RARELY PROFOUNDLY . . . NO ONE IS PERMITTED TO MAKE MENTION OF ANYTHING SAID OR DONE IN ANY OF THESE SITTINGS TO THOSE WHO MAY HAVE ATTENDED ANOTHER; FOR PARTY SPIRIT AND MISCHIEF MIGHT BE THE RESULT. TWENTY MINUTES OF THE UNION HOUR MAY BE DEVOTED TO THE SINGING OF SACRED SONGS IF DESIRED.

Clearly, although devotion was demanded, it was not to be a cause of factionalism within the sect itself. Everything in the Millennial Laws was designed to prevent the forming of attachments that might rock the increasingly stable Shaker boat. Thus it was contrary to the Millennial Laws of 1821 for members of a Family to stop to converse on 'broad' stairs in the streets or on walks for longer than was necessary to deliver a message or carry out an errand or enquire after the welfare of another brother or sister. Furthermore, the Millennial Laws also vetoed the growth and consolidation of particular friendships among Believers, and prevented the manufacturing of special presents for favoured brothers and sisters.

What was it, then, that held the Shakers together as a sect? All of the 'natural' avenues for the consolidation of a society had been suspended in favour of an imposed, yet readily accepted communism enforced by strict laws and a Millennialist faith in the power of Mother Ann. The Shakers' very separation from the outside world meant that, to an extent, they were forced to band together in order to survive. Legislation passed in New York State in 1818 proclaimed that any citizen who became a member of the Shaker movement would be considered 'civilly dead' for the purposes of the state. Any effects left behind after his removal from normal society would be disposed of as if he had actually died. Clearly, the legislative powers of the state departments were trying to stabilize the growing and independent Americas. Often the Shakers were regarded as a sect of predominantly European origin, one reason, therefore, that they were mistrusted.

It was not until the industries for which the Shakers were to gain limited fame began to enter into trade with the world at large that the Shakers came to be associated with trustworthiness and dependability rather than encountering the suspicion and doubt which they had first aroused. Perhaps it was in an attempt to cultivate that trust and understanding among the world's people that the Shakers threw open their doors for the Sunday worship and allowed the spectacle of their devotions to become something of a tourist attraction. Indeed, the meeting house at New Lebanon

ABOVE *A removable signpost designed to declare Shaker villages off limits to passers-by on Sundays, a day of rest and worship.*

OPPOSITE *A Shaker-style pantry at the Fruitlands Museum at Harvard, Massachusetts. The pantry and the kitchen was the focus for the daily work of most Shaker sisters.*

had been constructed to accommodate up to 1,000 outsiders. Initial reactions to first-hand experience of Shaker worship ranged from derision to heartfelt approbation. Certainly the spectacle of 500 Shakers marching in unison to the sound of the unaccompanied voices of the principal singers was a stirring sight, and the worship was lent a new solemnity by the changes wrought by Joseph Meacham. The scorn and derision that had sometimes been heaped on the Shakers was generally the response to the more extreme manifestations of seizure by the spirit world – what the Shakers termed 'coming under operations'. Meacham insisted on the introduction of a more uniform set of dances, which had been revealed to him in a vision. In keeping with the idea that Shaker life was the mirror image of heavenly existence, these new, simple dances were the earthly manifestation of the way in which the angels danced around the throne of God. Shakers willingly embraced the new steps, which involved a simple forward and backward marching movement, bowing or bending, and some 'turning' and shuffling steps. The hands would be held in front of the body – palms down to dispense blessings, palms up to gather blessings. In this way Shaker worship promoted equality among its participants: all Shaker brothers and sisters were able to practise the steps for the sake of harmony and equality in worship.

However, while the movements in their dance were rationalized, the unpredictable, spiritualist element of their worship never left the Shakers. As spiritualists, the Shakers believed in their ability to communicate with the spiritual world, and this ability manifested itself in the usual way in the mediums or 'instruments' through which the spirits chose to communicate with the Believers. Recipients of 'gifts' would display the signs of coming under operations, ie shaking, speaking in tongues and convulsing. Harvey Elkins describes the process in his *Fifteen Years in the Senior order of Shakers*:

TURNING RAPIDLY ON THE TOES, BOWING, BENDING, TWISTING AND REELING LIKE ONE A VICTIM TO THE FUMES OF INTOXICATION; SWOONING AND LYING PROSTRATE WITH LIMBS STIFF AND UNYIELDING LIKE A CORPSE AND TO ALL OUTWARD APPEARANCE THE VITAL SPARK EXTINCT; THEN SUDDENLY RESUSCITATING AND RISING TO JOIN IN THE JUBILANCY OF THE DANCE IN COMPANY WITH AND IN IMITATION OF THE ANGELS AROUND THE THRONE OF GOD.

For some outsiders, the spiritualism which was such a part of Shaker worship was difficult to comprehend, and only served to mystify further just what the Shakers were about. Between the years 1837 and 1844, the Shaker communities closed their doors

**LEFT** *A Shaker sister would spend much of her day cooking for the bretheren, who worked in the fields, workshops and manufactories. The Sisters would often cater for upwards of 200 hungry Shakers at a time.*

to the outside world, claiming an intensifying of spiritual activity which they termed Mother Ann's Work. This extraordinary period in the Shakers' history served to heighten still further the mystique of the sect, while confirming to the Shakers their true status on earth: that of a chosen people, destined to witness the end of the millennium. It was during this time that the gift to receive messages from heaven in the native tongues of the angels first manifested itself. These phonetic outpourings were incomprehensible to any one but the 'instruments', but were nonetheless important as they confirmed the close relationship that the Shakers had with the spirit world. The Millennial Hymns contain a gift song entitled 'Heavenly Guide'. One of its verses illustrates the nature of the 'gift to speak and sing in tongues':

> Lo all vo, Hark ye dear children and listen to me.
> For I am that holy se lone ka ra an ve
> My work on earth is holy, holy and pure
> That work which will ever, forever endure.

Later, these gift songs would be combined with the marching dances and demonstrated to the public when the Shaker worship came back into the world in 1844.

Apart from the aberrations in normal existence caused by the receiving of gifts from the spirit world, Shaker life followed an ordered pattern from day-to-day. Brothers and sisters were to be content with their lives, which, in general, were lived free from the uncertainty of fashion, debt and worldly preoccupations. They rose at half-past four in the summer and at five in the winter. Upon rising they would commence their chores. Two chairs would be placed in the centre of the retiring room, and the bedclothes would be stripped and laid across their backs with the pillows placed on the seats. The brethren would then remove the slops while the sisters remade the beds and swept the floor. Breakfast would be at half-past six, dinner at twelve, supper at six in the evening, and the dwelling house would be quiet with all the occupants asleep by nine or half-past at the latest.

The period between the end of supper and retiring was set aside as either recreational or devotional time. A typical Shaker week at New (Mount) Lebanon in 1879 would designate this period for use as follows: On Monday evenings a general meeting would be held, with reading from newspapers. Stories concerning crime and accidents were omitted from the reading, being thought of as 'unprofitable to spirit and constitution'. Letters from other societies would also be read at this time. Tuesday evenings were spent

**ABOVE** *Other Shaker sisters would teach the adopted Shaker children in specially built schoolhouses. Shaker schools were recognised by the central government of the US as being of a superior standard to similar schools of the day, both in terms of the facilities offered and in the standard of teaching.*

**LEFT** *Sister's bonnet on a chair, originally made in Canterbury, New Hampshire, and now in the Shaker Museum, Old Chatham, New York.*

**ABOVE** *Cloaks as worn by the Shaker sisters in the winter months.*

in worship and marching. Wednesdays were reserved for the union meetings. On Thursdays a religious service would be held, and Fridays saw the time set aside for the learning of new songs and hymns. On Saturday evening there would be more dancing and singing, and Sundays would see brethren and sisters visit each others rooms for singing and conversation. This would be done by appointment only, and visits were chaperoned by the presence of other brethren and sisters. These evenings must have been a welcome break after spending the day in the 'shops' or fields.

Although the day would be taken up with work, it would be a mistake to assume that the Shakers toiled. Rather they laboured steadily and slowly, making sure that quality was maintained in the goods produced. With their denial of the worldly way to riches and success the Shakers never saw themselves as being in competition with anyone. Therefore any work which needed to be done was met with sufficient hands, and with a willingness based on the secure knowledge that every brother and sister was labouring for the common good.

Everyday Shaker life was characterized and conditioned by the maintenance of segregation from the world on a spiritual level and by increasing interaction with the world when it came to business and financial transactions. The reputation enjoyed by the Shakers was generally one of reliability, honesty and fairness in their business dealings, but the 'Shaker constitution' did not allow for the consolidation and expansion of their business interests beyond that which was strictly necessary for their survival. However, there were exceptions to this general principle. One of the most notorious examples is the story of Caleb Dyer, who in 1813 had joined the Shakers at the age of 13. By the age of 24, he was Assistant Trustee to the Church Family at Enfield, New Hampshire. By the time he was 38, he had attained the position of 1st Trustee and was able to oversee the expenditure of over $35,000 on the granite dwelling house. The comparative wealth of this community was increased by the founding of the flannel mills in 1841. Under Dyer the community expanded its interests by buying into railroad stock, which was capitalized upon by the building of a sawmill near the railway line. A four-storey machine shop was then built in granite for the Church Family, while the North Family erected a brick-built office block in 1850. The previous year had seen the completion of a bridge by Shaker mechanics, and in 1854 the great barn was raised for the South Family. Two years later the foundations for a grist mill were laid and the river was dammed to provide the power source. That same year the flannel factory was extended and the three largest taxpayers for the region were recorded as Dyer (Church Family),

Samuel Beaker (South Family) and True W. Heath (North Family). Such was the success of the Shaker movement in the town of Enfield that at one point the townspeople attempted to change the name to Dyersville; characteristically this move was resisted by the Shaker elders. The Shaker mills company was eventually taken over by A. Conant and Co, after the company had overextended on credit to its customers and then got into financial difficulty. Caleb Dyer was shot in 1863 by an anonymous but interested party, and died three days after the incident leaving no accurate records or accounts. The ensuing court case over the disputed ownership of the mills dragged on for 20 years, and at its close the Shakers of Enfield emerged some $20,000 poorer.

**BELOW** *A reconstruction of a Shaker workroom at the Fruitlands Museum, Harvard, Massachusetts.*

**LEFT** *The Herb Garden at Sabbathday Lake, Maine, still produces and sells the dried herbs which were such a part of both Shaker cuisine and commerce.*

That Caleb Dyer had kept no records or accounts save for those contained in a small book and rendered in his own shorthand was not unusual. The Shaker approach to their communal lifestyle meant that, in the words of elder E.W. Evans, 'we will [never] make nor require any account of any interest, property, labor or service which has been or which may be devoted by us or any of us to the purposes aforesaid'. The 'purposes aforesaid' were phrased as 'the natural protection, support, comfort and happiness of each other as Brethren and Sisters in the Gospel'. In many other communities accounts, journals and records were kept, but the Shakers at Enfield placed all of the trust in their financial well-being in the hands of Caleb Dyer; and while he cannot be said to have abused that trust, the over-expansion of Shaker interests eventually led to his downfall. Where the Shaker communities worked, they were seen to work exceedingly well, and they even served to illustrate to Friedrich Engels, the co-founder of Marxist Communism, that the secular side of Shaker life constituted proof that the premises of communism were operable. Unsurprisingly, Engels found difficulty in reconciling the mystical and religious sides of Shaker life with what he saw as the model for successful living of a communistic life. To the Shakers these two sides of life were indivisible.

The Shakers' egalitarian approach to life, work and worship was based directly on their theology. Because they saw God as an entity consisting of male and female parts in completely equal symbiosis, and in keeping with the idea that the Shakers were the earthly manifestation of heavenly life, women in the Shaker movement were accorded the same status as the men. In terms of the sexual politics of the 18th and 19th centuries these were radical ideas indeed. The patriarchal dictates and traditions of 'the world' were overturned by the belief that Mother Ann had represented the second coming of Christ in female form. Equality therefore extended into everything from the value of work to the responsibility of each individual to their Family. The fact that bodies such as ministries and bishoprics comprised both men and women, each with an equal say in the government and regulation of the brethren and sisters, speaks volumes about the advanced nature of some aspects of Shaker society. The abnegation of all sexual practices can be seen to have been at the root of the redefinition of power relations between the sexes within the Shaker world; however, it is worth bearing in mind that, of those Shakers who went out into the world to carry the Gospel, justify their existence or conduct themselves in trade, by far the majority were men, such as Caleb Dyer and Frederick W. Evans.

The Shakers existed as an enclave of ideals in a world of rapidly changing standards, technologies and behaviours. In their dealings with 'the world' they were bound by worldly conventions and influenced by worldly misdeeds. Within Shaker society, where their values and ideas were seen to count for the most, the binding together of life, work and worship into a philosophically and theologically motivated holistic existence was to prove successful for well over 150 years.

**BELOW** *Farming and outdoor activities played a large part in the Shaker economy and way of life.*

**RIGHT** *White-painted fencing such as this was widely used around Shaker dwellings and work buildings.*

# 6

## THE ART
## OF THE
## SHAKERS

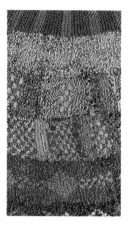

**LEFT** *Farm buildings at*
*Hancock, Massachusetts,*
*at dawn.*

**ABOVE** *A view of Hancock, with its unusual Brick Dwelling and tannery.*

The things that came out of the Shaker 'shops' and manufactories were not created as 'art objects'. The earliest chairs, tools, pill makers and candlesticks were conceived out of necessity as objects of utility, whose creation was governed by the maxims left to the makers by their beloved Mother Ann – 'Put your hands to work and your hearts to God', 'Beauty rests in utility', and so on. The Shaker object as art object is an almost mythological idea, which has grown up around the Shakers and their work as we look back to their altruistic and utopian lifestyle from the hurly burly of the 20th century; the transcendent qualities of the Shaker object are for us the touchstones of what we perceive as a simpler way of life. Shaker objects began to attain status as art objects because they became fashionable, first in the 1860s and again in the 1930s. As a result of the interest of 'the world' they became locked into the value systems that promote things of age as desirable and expensive status symbols. In consequence the auction house and museum have sanctified the Shaker aesthetic and elevated it to the status of art in direct contradiction to the spirit in which much of Shaker design was originally conceived. While the Shakers wanted and needed no part in fashion, the world of art is as susceptible to the vagaries of fashionable whim as any other institution that deals in objects as commodities. What is it, then, that has caused these essentially humble objects to be accorded such status in the modern world?

The Shakers and their approach to the design of their lives found favour with many contemporary observers. Robert Owen, the Welsh reformer who had dreamed of working men cooperating in industrial production, took many ideas from the organization of the Shaker communities, which he visited in the early 19th century. His cotton-spinning factory at New Lanark in Scotland was a celebrated workers' co-operative; but it was an organizational

**RIGHT** *A late 19th-century Shaker basket displaying all the Shaker hallmarks of propriety, utility and consummate skill in manufacture and design.*

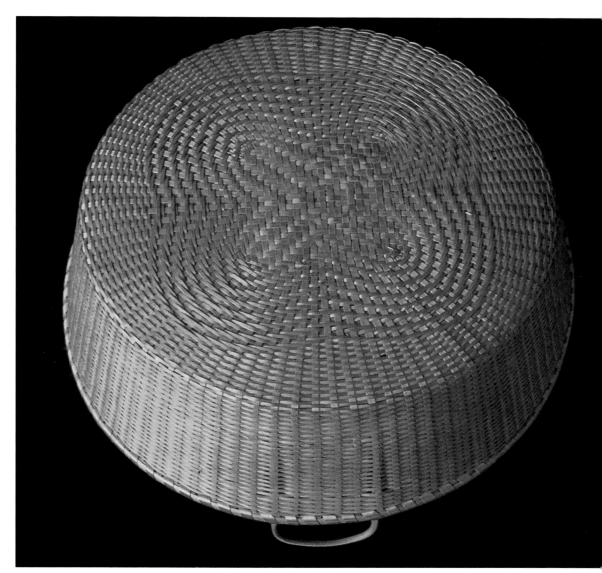

rather than an aesthetic inspiration that Owen derived from his experience of Shaker life and production. Rather a different kind of debt was owed to the Shakers by the American Arts and Crafts Movement, which blossomed on the East Coast during the 1880s; the Shakers happened to be a ready-made domestic example of the Arts and Crafts ethos advocated by William Morris, John Ruskin and C.R. Ashbee in Great Britain. Ironically, it was the Engilsh Arts and Crafts ideal that eventually found greater currency with the American public, after the brief flare in the popularity of the Shaker idiom in New York in the 1860s. The English Arts and Crafts movement was a celebration of traditional craftsmanship, and it advocated an approach to design and manufacture that was in many ways similar to that of the Shakers. John Ruskin, a prime mover in the spreading of the Arts and Crafts ideal, was an influence on Gustav Stickley, who in turn generated a classic

**BELOW** *A Shaker carding machine for combing and separating strands of wool before spinning. The emphasis on self sufficiency in the Shaker way of life meant that, if possible, all machinery was made in the Shaker workshops by the Shaker bretheren.*

LEFT *A hand-knitted circular mat, possibly for sale to the outside world.*

American style which has also become fashionable. The Shaker aesthetic has much in common with these styles and so has been connected with them.

The aesthetic which grew out of the Shaker way of life became a tradition for Shakers and is now an accepted part of American material culture. Where the aesthetic is brought together in its most complete form, in the meeting houses and retiring rooms or in the simplest of early Shaker chairs, the effect can indeed be transcendent of the ordinary and the utilitarian. The Shakers professed to have no use for beauty preferring instead to describe it as 'utility'. But there is beauty in that very utility, and in the perfection of the craftsmanship that was applied to all Shaker creations. At their best, things made by the Shakers exist beyond the world of fashion and have a timeless quality about them that will ensure their survival as relics of a past utopia. One Shaker sister was heard to remark 'I don't want to be remembered as a stick of furniture'. However, it *is* those old sticks of furniture, together with surviving buildings, that remain as testament to the Shaker way of life.

125

# INDEX

*Note: Illustrations are indicated by italics. Sometimes there are also textual references on these pages.*

## PICTURE CREDITS
## AND ACKNOWLEDGEMENTS

### THE PHOTOGRAPHS IN THIS BOOK WERE TAKEN BY

**MICHAEL FREEMAN** (pp 1, 2, 5, 6, 12, 14, 15, 21, 28, 31, 35, 41, 44, 47, 49, 56, 59, 64, 65, 67, 68, 70, 72, 75, 76, 77, 78, 80, 81, 82, 83, 84, 85, 86, 87, 89, 91, 93, 94, 97, 98, 100, 101, 102, 104, 106, 107, 109, 111, 113, 114, 115, 116, 118 and 120)

and **PAUL ROCHELEAU** (pp 3, 7, 8, 10, 11, 14, 15, 23, 24, 25, 30, 32, 33, 34, 35, 38, 39, 40, 42, 43, 45, 46, 50, 51, 52, 54, 57, 58, 60, 61, 62, 63, 65, 71, 73, 74, 87, 89, 90, 92, 95, 96, 99, 100, 105, 110, 112, 113, 121, 122, 123, 124 and 125)

with other contributions from the **MARY EVANS PICTURE LIBRARY** (pp 16, 17, 18, 20 and 88) and the American Museum at Bath (pp 36 and 37).

Thanks also to the **WESTERN RESERVE HISTORICAL SOCIETY**, Cleveland, Ohio for use of the spirit drawing on page 25, and to the collection of the Darrow School for the alphabet board on page 10.